EXPLORING

ANCIENT

CIVILIZATIONS

9

Roads – Sports and Entertainment

Marshall Cavendish

Sydney

Marshall Cavendish
99 White Plains Road
Tarrytown, New York 10591-9001

www.marshallcavendish.com

Consultants: Daud Ali, School of Oriental and African
Studies, University of London; Michael Brett, School
of Oriental and African Studies, London; John
Chinnery, School of Oriental and African Studies,
London; Philip de Souza; Joann Fletcher; Anthony
Green; Peter Groff, Department of Philosophy,
Bucknell University; Mark Handley, History
Department, University College London; Anders
Karlsson, School of Oriental and African Studies,
London; Alan Leslie, Glasgow University Archaeology
Research Department; Michael E. Smith, Department
of Anthropology, University at Albany; Matthew
Spriggs, Head of School of Archaeology and
Anthropology, Australian National University

Contributing authors: Richard Balkwill, Richard
Burrows, Peter Chrisp, Richard Dargie, Steve Eddy,
Clive Gifford, Jen Green, Peter Hicks, Robert Hull,
Jonathan Ingoldby, Pat Levy, Steven Maddocks, John
Malam, Saviour Pirotta, Stewart Ross, Sean Sheehan,
Jane Shuter

WHITE-THOMSON PUBLISHING
Editors: Alex Woolf, Tamara Colloff-Bennett, and
Steven Maddocks
Design: Derek Lee
Cartographer: Peter Bull Design
Picture Research: Glass Onion Pictures
Indexer: Fiona Barr

MARSHALL CAVENDISH
Editor: Thomas McCarthy
Editorial Director: Paul Bernabeo
Production Manager: Michael Esposito

Library of Congress Cataloging-in-Publication Data
Exploring ancient civilizations.
    p. cm.
Includes bibliographical references and indexes.
   ISBN 0-7614-7456-0 (set : alk. paper) -- ISBN 0-7614-7457-9 (v. 1 :
alk. paper) -- ISBN 0-7614-7458-7 (v. 2 : alk. paper) -- ISBN
0-7614-7459-5 (v. 3 : alk. paper) -- ISBN 0-7614-7460-9 (v. 4 : alk.
paper) -- ISBN 0-7614-7461-7 (v. 5 : alk. paper) -- ISBN 0-7614-7462-5
(v. 6 : alk. paper) -- ISBN 0-7614-7463-3 (v. 7 : alk. paper) -- ISBN
0-7614-7464-1 (v. 8 : alk. paper) -- ISBN 0-7614-7465-X (v. 9 : alk.
paper) -- ISBN 0-7614-7466-8 (v. 10 : alk. paper) -- ISBN 0-7614-7467-6
(v. 11 : alk. paper)
   1. Civilization, Ancient--Encyclopedias.
   CB311.E97 2004
   930'.03--dc21

                                    2003041224

ISBN 0-7614-7456-0 (set)
ISBN 0-7614-7465-X (vol. 9)

Printed and bound in China

07 06 05 04 03 5 4 3 2 1

ILLUSTRATION CREDITS

AKG London: 646 (Pirozzi), 647 (Hilbich), 648, 649 (Pirozzi), 650 (Erich Lessing), 651
(Erich Lessing), 652 (Erich Lessing), 653 (Erich Lessing), 657 (Erich Lessing), 659, 660,
662 (Erich Lessing), 664, 667 (Erich Lessing), 668 (Erich Lessing), 669 (Erich Lessing),
672 (Jean-Louis Nou), 673 (Jean-Louis Nou), 676, 677, 679, 682 (Erich Lessing), 685
(British Library, London), 690 (Erich Lessing), 693 (Erich Lessing), 694 (Erich Lessing),
701 (Erich Lessing), 704, 707 (Erich Lessing), 708 (Erich Lessing), 711 (John Hios),
713.
Ancient Art and Architecture Collection: 675, 691 (Ronald Sheridan).
The Art Archive: 710.
Bridgeman Art Library: 644 (Ashmolean Museum, Oxford), 645 (Temple of Luxor,
Egypt), 654 (Museo del Settecento, Venice), 655, 663, 674 (Musée d'Orsay, Paris), 680
(Bonhams, London), 683 (British Museum, London), 695 (Musée du Louvre, Paris), 696
(Birmingham Museums and Art Gallery, UK), 705 (Archives Charmet), 706, 714
(Giraudon), 715 (Ashmolean Museum, Oxford), 716 (Ca' d'Oro, Venice), 718.
British Library, London: 671.
British Museum, London: 670.
C. M. Dixon: 700.
Corbis: 699 (Roger Wood).
Joann Fletcher: 703.
Mary Evans Picture Library: 684.
Werner Forman Archive: 658, 661, 666, 681 (British Museum, London), 687 (The
Hermitage Museum, St. Petersburg, Russia), 688 (The Hermitage Museum, St.
Petersburg, Russia), 692 (Cheops Barque Museum, Giza, Egypt), 697, 698, 702 (British
Museum, London), 717.

Contents

Roads

In the ancient world roads were built only by powerful regimes with considerable wealth, such as those of Persia, Rome, China, and the Mauryan Empire. Good roads, as the prime enablers of trade, were a source of incalculable benefit to a society. The Roman road system, the best in the ancient world, was crucial to the commercial and military success of the Roman Empire.

The first civilizations developed without roads. Although streets ran through towns and cities, beyond the walls was just a network of trails. In a dry climate, like that of Egypt, the lack of constructed roads made little difference. However, in places that had heavy rainfall, such as Europe and northern India, overland travel in wet weather was difficult, and people preferred to undertake long journeys by water.

This situation changed dramatically toward the end of the fourth millennium BCE with the invention of the wheeled cart. Carts traveling across a piece of land soon churn up the surface and make it impassable. The solution was to build a solid platform for carts and travelers to move along—in other words, a road.

Symbols of Power

The construction of the first roads reveals a great deal about the civilizations that undertook such work.

To build a highway of any length, the government had to control large numbers of laborers—usually slaves. It had to be powerful enough to overcome local objections to the project. The construction of a road was undertaken only by sophisticated supervisors. They not only put the road in place but also planned the whole operation and maintained the road once it had been built. Such supervisors also needed to have the foresight to recognize the road's many purposes and benefits.

A great road was a symbol of royal power. The Persian royal road, for example, was over 1,600 miles (2,575 km) long. Built in the sixth century BCE, it ran from Ephesus on the Aegean Sea to Susa, near the head of the Persian Gulf.

A good road system, such as that of the Mauryan Empire, was also a great commercial asset. An increase in trade made citizens wealthier; they in turn could provide rulers with greater tax revenue.

▼ This terra-cotta model of a covered wagon, found near Carchemish in Turkey, dates from around 2400 BCE and gives an indication of how the earliest wheeled vehicles may have looked.

Latest News

Roads enabled royal messengers to carry news and orders great distances at high speed. According to historical accounts, a Persian courier traveling the royal road could cover a distance of 1,678 miles (2,700 km) in one week—although he was obliged to change horses continually. Fresh horses were kept in royal stables along the route.

Roads and Soldiers

Roads were of key military importance, too. A well-constructed network of roads enabled troops to move swiftly and easily to wherever they were required. The Romans built a network of almost 50,000 miles (80,500 km) of expertly laid-out roads. This distance is equal to twice the circumference of the earth.

ROADS IN CHINA

The Chinese developed the wheel around 2000 BCE, and road construction began not long afterward. The Chinese imperial road system eventually linked all of the major cities of the empire. By 200 BCE the system's total length was 4,250 miles (6,840 km), and by 200 CE China's road network totaled 20,000 miles (32,186 km).

▲ Built by the Egyptian pharaoh Amenhotep III (reigned c. 1390–1352 BCE), this sphinx-lined avenue is three miles (5 km) long and connects the temple at Karnak to the one at Luxor.

By the second century CE it was theoretically possible for a Roman legion to march on paved roads all the way from Hadrian's Wall in northern England to Egypt or Mesopotamia (though it would have to be ferried across the English Channel and the Bosporus).

The Construction of Ancient Roads

Early civilizations used several different techniques of road construction. The simplest was suited to dry, stony, or desert regions, such as Egypt and central Persia, where the ground was naturally hard. This type of road building consisted simply of clearing large stones to make a level pathway. In regions where the soil was softer and the rainfall higher, engineers were more careful. On Europe's Amber Route, for instance, builders gave the road solidity by placing logs lengthways and crossways across marshy stretches.

In India the foundation of the road was built up with stone or other hard material wherever possible. The roads that ran along the Indus valley were paved with bricks held together with bitumen (a kind of tar that is extracted from rock). As this method allowed water to drain off the surface of the road, it prevented the road from being washed away. Whatever the surface, roads had to be regularly maintained. Repairs included building up sections washed away in rains, filling in potholes, and leveling the tracks left by cart wheels. Without leveling, the road surface became rutted, and cart wheels were held in the grooves. Deep grooves damaged the wheels and made passing almost impossible.

The best-constructed roads of ancient times were those of the Romans, who also built the first stone bridges. One or two, such as the bridge at Rimini, Italy, are still in use. Most Roman bridges, such as the one that crossed the Thames at London, were built of wood. Outside the Roman Empire bridges were very rare. By far the most common way of crossing a river was by ford.

▶ The Pons Aemilius (now named the Ponte Rotto) bridges the Tiber River in Rome. Completed in 142 CE, it was the first walled bridge.

▲ *The Ostia Antica leads from Rome to the port of Ostia, 19 miles (30 km) away.*

Roman Roads

The Romans were the first people to base road building on the principles of engineering. Roman roads were planned very carefully, and as a result, their roads lasted hundreds of years. Many examples survive to the present time. Roman engineers showed their logical mastery by building roads as straight as nature would allow. The highway's hard surface of packed lava or stones was curved to allow water to run off. There were three layers beneath the surface, reaching to a depth of about three feet (about 1 m): a mix of gravel and lime, rows of flat stones, and at the base, a foundation of sand or mortar.

FOR AS LONG AS ROADS HAVE BEEN BUILT, WRITERS HAVE COMPARED LIFE TO A JOURNEY ALONG A ROAD. THE METAPHOR OF THE ROAD OF LIFE WAS ESPECIALLY POPULAR IN ANCIENT CHINESE POETRY. THE FOLLOWING EXAMPLE IS BY THE POET TU FU (712–770 CE):

By Yangtse and Han the mountains pile their barriers.
A cloud in the wind, at the corner of the world.
Year in, year out, there's no familiar thing,
And stop after stop is the end of my road. . . .
My heart in peaceful times had cracked already,
And I walk a road each day more desolate.

TU FU, *AT THE CORNER OF THE WORLD*

SEE ALSO

• China • Cities • Roman Republic and Empire
• Trade • Transportation

Roman Mythology

Roman mythology is the patchwork of stories, generally involving fantastical or magical elements, through which the Romans expressed some of their beliefs about their religion and their history. Roman myths were often based on earlier stories. These stories were gathered from all over the Roman Empire, especially from Greece, and because they were developed and recorded in Roman literature and poetry, myths from throughout the Roman Empire survive to this day.

Greek Mythology and the Romans

The Romans adopted many of the Greek gods, sometimes identifying them with gods of their own. For example, Zeus, the chief god of the Greeks, was identified with Jupiter, the Roman god of the skies.

The Romans took into their culture not only the Greek gods but also all the many stories that the Greeks had been telling about their gods. Through the myths of their gods, the Greeks had sought to explain how the world had been made and what man's role on earth was. Greek myths answered questions such as why there were seasons and how fire came about. The Romans adopted these myths along with the gods.

The Romans, however, associated very few stories with their own gods. Rather, the gods were simply figures that represented certain powers—the sky and thunderbolts in the case of Jupiter, for example.

Many Roman myths are nonreligious. They answer historical questions, such as how Rome was established and what the early years of the city were like.

Romulus and Remus

The story of Romulus and Remus is one of the most famous historical myths of the Romans. Romulus and Remus were the twin sons of Rhea Silva and the god Mars. Rhea's uncle Amulius had killed Rhea's father. He did not want Rhea to have any children, and when the twins were born, he cast them into the river. However, they floated downstream to the spot where Rome would one day be built, and a female

▶ The head of a bronze statue of Zeus, father of the Greek gods.

wolf found them and suckled them. Later a shepherd discovered the twin boys and brought them up.

When the boys grew up, they avenged their grandfather by killing Amulius and then founded the new city of Rome. Romulus invited people to live in his city and also stole the wives of a neighboring tribe, the Sabines, in order to increase Rome's population. He built a wall around his city and decreed that no one could breach the wall. Remus did not know about the decree, and one day he jumped over the wall. A man named Celer, acting on Romulus's instructions, killed Remus.

After some time Romulus seems to have disappeared. The Romans came to believe that he had been made into the god Quirinus.

IN THE *AENEID*, THE ROMAN POET VIRGIL DESCRIBES THE WOLF AND THE TWIN BOYS ROMULUS AND REMUS:

He had also wrought there the tale of the wolf
which after littering had stretched herself on the ground
in the green cave of Mars with twin baby boys playing
  around her . . .
while she, bending her smooth neck round and round,
  caressed each in its turn
and licked their limbs into shape.

VIRGIL, *AENEID*, BOOK I

▼ This late-fifth-century-BCE bronze Etruscan statue shows the infants Romulus and Remus being fed by the she-wolf.

The Sibyl of Cumae and Tarquin

The story of the sibyl of Cumae, a priestess who could tell the future, is probably a myth, but it may contain some truth. The sibyl offered to sell nine books of prophecies to Tarquin, a Roman tyrant. Hoping to bargain with her, Tarquin refused, and the sibyl threw three of the books onto the fire. She then offered him the remaining six books at the same price. Again he refused, and again she threw three books onto the fire. Finally the sibyl offered the last three books at the original price, and this time Tarquin accepted the offer. This story may have arisen to explain the origins of the three ancient books of prophecies that were kept in the temple of Jupiter in Rome and that were consulted in times of emergency.

Original Roman Gods

Several of Rome's earliest gods were not imported. One of them, Saturn, the god of sowing and the father of Jupiter, was worshiped in Roman times during the Saturnalia festival, held in late December. Faunus, the god of fields and of shepherds, is another Roman god with no Greek equivalent. Other non-Greek Roman gods and goddesses are Bellona, a war goddess; Terminus, the god of boundaries; Volturnus, the god of the Tiber River; and Voltumna, the god of kindness and goodwill.

The Romans had gods for almost every aspect of life, from events such as birth and death to places such as woods and lakes and even trivia such as household doors and mildew. These gods were *numina*, spirits that permeated a particular place or a particular moment. Very few myths or stories about them survive.

Later Imports from Other Cultures

Other gods derived from other cultures. Cybele, who originated in Phrygia in modern central Turkey, was the goddess of nature and the mother of all the gods. The Greeks associated her with Rhea, Zeus's mother, and the Romans named her Magna Mater (great mother). There are many stories, or myths, associated with her. None of them are Roman in origin, but the Romans took her and myths about her as their own. Other well-known imports are Isis from Egypt and Mithras from Persia.

▼ This relief statue, carved in sandstone, dates to the third century CE. It shows a priest in Roman dress making a sacrificial offering at an altar to the goddess Cybele.

OVID'S METAMORPHOSES

One story in Ovid's Metamorphoses *is the Babylonian tale of Pyramus and Thisbe, two lovers who run away from their families in order to be together. They lose one another in a wood, and Pyramus kills himself. When Thisbe finds him under a mulberry tree, she, too, commits suicide. Since that day the fruit of some mulberry trees has been black instead of white.*

Another story tells of Echo, a nymph who annoyed the goddess Hera. Hera took away her ability to speak, and all that Echo could do was repeat the last few words that were spoken to her. She fell in love with a youth named Narcissus and pined away until only her voice was left in the mountains.

◀ The story of Narcissus and Echo, recorded by Ovid in his Metamorphoses, *is the subject of this early-seventeenth-century painting by Nicolas Poussin.*

Mythology in Roman Literature

While many educated Roman writers appear to be sceptical about the stories of the gods, Roman poets used mythology in their writing. The poet Virgil wrote the *Aeneid* in order to glorify the state of Rome by telling the mythical story of its birth. Later Ovid took all the myths he knew of that were concerned with magical changes and wove them into his long poem *Metamorphoses*. It is from this work that many of the Greek and Roman myths are known. *Metamorphoses* remains one of the most influential works of Roman literature.

SEE ALSO
• Aeneid
• Egyptian Mythology
• Greek Mythology
• Religion
• Rome, City of

Roman Philosophy

Roman philosophy was based largely on the ideas of the Greek philosophers. Roman philosophers adopted many Greek ideas, particularly from the Greek schools of thought known as Stoicism and Epicureanism. The works of the Greek philosopher Aristotle also greatly influenced Roman thought. Another Roman philosophical system, Neoplatonism, which arose toward the end of the Roman Empire, went back to the ideas of the Greek philosopher Plato.

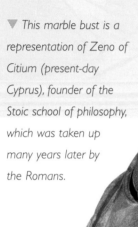

▼ *This marble bust is a representation of Zeno of Citium (present-day Cyprus), founder of the Stoic school of philosophy, which was taken up many years later by the Romans.*

Stoicism

Stoicism was first proposed in about 300 BCE by Zeno, who was born in Cyprus. Zeno lost all his fortunes at sea and went to Athens to study philosophy. He began teaching his own thoughts in a building called the Stoa Poikile (from which the name Stoicism comes).

To Zeno and the philosophers who followed his ideas, all the material things in life, such as wealth and power, and all strong feelings, such as love or rage, were distractions. What mattered was being virtuous—brave, wise, and just. Stoics believed a person should live in harmony with nature. A person's fate was inevitable because it was governed by divine law, and so hardships should be patiently endured.

Stoicism in Rome

The ideas of the Stoics were taken up in Roman times in the second century BCE, a time when Rome was undergoing civil war, slave rebellions, and intrigues in the senate. The Romans of the republican era believed a man should have *virtus*—a combination of wisdom, self-discipline, and a sense of honor. This view of life fitted very well with that of the Stoics.

When the Roman Republic was overturned by Julius Caesar and then Augustus, who

SENECA C. 4 BCE–65 CE

Seneca was one of the most important Roman Stoics. His life and writings gave Stoicism, which could be a very cold philosophy, a human face. As a young man Seneca studied philosophy and then became a lawyer and politician. He was twice sentenced to death and twice pardoned. Around 49 CE he became friendly with Agrippina, the wife of the emperor Claudius.

Agrippina gave Seneca the job of tutoring her son, the future emperor Nero. When Nero came to power, Seneca was his chief adviser and helped the young Nero to make many reforms in Rome and the colonies. Later Nero came to resent the influence of his advisers, and so Seneca retired from Rome to write books of philosophy. Seneca's Stoicism helped him endure a life of great tragedy—a life that ended when Nero forced him to commit suicide.

▼ A portrait, painted in 1476, of Seneca, whose books about Stoic philosophy influenced philosophers for many hundreds of years after his death.

ruled as emperors, the ideas of Stoicism were taken up by those men who preferred republican government. One of them was Cato, a leading senator who committed suicide rather than live under the rule of Julius Caesar.

Later, Stoicism became popular with more of the leading men in Rome. Seneca, who advised the young emperor Nero, was a Stoic. The emperor Marcus Aurelius wrote books of Stoic philosophy.

Epicureanism

Both Epicureanism and Stoicism seek the same object—how to be a good person. However, the ideas and methods of Epicureanism are very different from those of Stoicism. Epicureanism originated with the Greek philosopher Epicurus. His school, which was opened in Athens in 306 BCE, was the first to admit women. Epicureanism was in a sense the opposite of Stoicism. To Epicureans the pursuit of personal happiness was the most important thing, and Epicureans believed happiness could be found only by withdrawing from society and taking pleasure in the simplest things in life.

ANNAEO·SENECAE·CCR

Epicureanism in Rome

Originally the Epicureans recommended withdrawal from public life to one of contemplation, friendship, and simplicity. However, some Romans distorted Epicurean ideas, and Epicureanism was denounced as an excuse for not believing in the gods, not working hard, and living only for pleasure. Those who actually read the works of the Epicureans knew that the charges against this philosophy were unfounded. Many of the principles of Epicureanism were taken up by Cicero, Seneca, and other influential men.

Philosophy in Roman Life

Wealthy Roman families believed that studying the ideas of the Greek philosophers was an essential part of the education of a young man. From republican times onward, noble Roman families employed Greek philosophers to teach their sons the elements of philosophy. Some young men even went to Athens to study in the schools of philosophy there. Most well-taught noblemen in Rome would at least have been familiar with the ideas of Plato, Aristotle, Stoicism, and Epicureanism.

The Romans found ideas that suited them and adapted them to their own needs. Cicero, for example, studied all four Greek schools of thought. In his own philosophical writings he included principles from all the schools to describe what a good country and a good life should be like. Cicero owed much to Aristotle's combination of reasoning and eloquence. Cicero himself said that his ideas were not original but that he was trying to provide a kind of encyclopedia for his countrymen.

Some of the Greek philosophers' ideas conflicted with Roman ideals. The Epicureans, for example, taught that one should withdraw from society to contemplate ideas. These teachings became so unpopular that Epicurean philosophers were actually banned from Rome twice, once in 173 BCE and again in 161.

Neoplatonism

In the third century CE some Roman philosophers, chiefly Plotinus and Porphyry, turned away from Christianity and back to the ancient Greek ideas of Plato. Their complex system of beliefs is known as Neoplatonism.

Neoplatonism proposes the existence of several levels of being. The highest is the good. The next level of being is the intellect, or reason, and the third is the soul. Beneath that level is everything that people can sense in the world. At the lowest level is matter, considered the cause of all evil. The goal is to move up from the base level of matter to the highest level and become one with the good.

In the fifth and sixth centuries, two events brought about a final decline in the influence of Neoplatonism, Stoicism, and Epicureanism: in 476 the Western Empire fell, and in 529 the emperor Justinian banned the teaching of non-Christian philosophies in the Eastern Empire.

▶ The Roman philosopher Plotinus, who lived from 205 to 270 CE, is regarded as the founder of Neoplatonism. At his school, discussion was unlimited, and questions, once raised, had to be solved.

SEE ALSO
• Aristotle • Greek Philosophy
• Marcus Aurelius • Plato

IN ONE OF HIS LETTERS TO HIS FRIEND LUCILLUS, SENECA WROTE ABOUT HIS ATTITUDE TOWARD LIFE AND LIVING:

When we are about to go to sleep, let us say in joyful cheerfulness: "I have lived; I have traveled the route that fortune has assigned me." If God should grant us tomorrow as well, let us accept it joyfully. That person is most happy and in calm possession of himself who waits for tomorrow without worries. Whoever says "I have lived," gets up every day to receive unexpected riches.

SENECA, *LETTERS TO LUCILLUS*

Roman Republic and Empire

The civilization of ancient Rome—a hill town that grew to be the seat of a kingdom, a republic, and an empire—endured for more than a thousand years. Though the Roman Republic collapsed, its ideals and institutions inspired the framers of the U.S. Constitution. At its height in about 117 CE, the Roman Empire extended from Britain to Egypt and from Spain to the Tigris and Euphrates Rivers. Until the collapse of the empire in the west in the fifth century, the impact of Roman power was felt through much of the known world.

Early History

In the tenth century BCE, Rome was a small village on the Palatine Hill in central Italy. By the sixth century the village had become a small town. From 753 to 509 BCE, Rome was ruled by kings, and the town gradually expanded until it had become a city covering seven hills. Tarquin, who was probably Etruscan, was Rome's last king. Historians believe that Tarquin was responsible for many of the early city's new buildings and roads.

▼ The Roman Empire at its greatest extent, around 120 CE.

ROMAN REPUBLIC AND EMPIRE

753 BCE

According to legend, Romulus and Remus found Rome.

509 BCE

Tarquin, the last king of Rome, is thrown out. The republic begins.

493 BCE

Rome establishes rule over other Latin cities.

264–241 BCE

War against Carthage.

218–202 BCE

Hannibal's armies attack Italy.

149–146 BCE

Final war against Carthage.

73 BCE

Spartacus leads a revolt of slaves.

45 BCE

Julius Caesar takes power in Rome.

27 BCE

Augustus becomes emperor.

43 CE

Emperor Claudius invades Britain.

64 CE

Much of Rome is destroyed by fire.

9 CE

Mount Vesuvius erupts and destroys Pompeii.

122–132 CE

Hadrian's Wall is constructed.

286 CE

Diocletian divides the empire.

330 CE

Constantine moves the capital to Byzantium.

410 CE

Rome is sacked.

476 CE

The last western emperor is deposed.

THE ROMAN ARMY

During the republican period the army consisted of male citizens who went to war as needed and afterward returned to their families. A man's wealth determined what kind of soldier he would be. The richest, who could afford a horse, formed the cavalry. The poorest were barred from serving because they could not afford weapons.

By the time of Augustus, the army was a permanent professional body of around 300,000 men. The core troop was a legion of between 3,000 and 6,000 legionaries. A legion was divided into smaller units known as cohorts. A legionary joined up for twenty years. He bought his own armor and food, but he was well paid and got a share of the loot after a battle. Legionaries often became provincial governors or senators in Rome. Under Augustus auxiliary soldiers—men from the provinces and marines stationed in the empire's ports— were granted Roman citizenship at the end of their term of duty. They were given land and could marry.

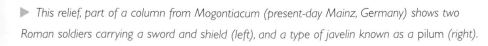

▶ *This relief, part of a column from Mogontiacum (present-day Mainz, Germany) shows two Roman soldiers carrying a sword and shield (left), and a type of javelin known as a pilum (right).*

▶ After Carthage was destroyed in 146 BCE, a Roman colony was established. This picture shows the remains of the Roman baths at Carthage. The pillars once supported the ceiling of the hypocaust, an open space in which hot air and smoke were circulated to heat the room above.

The Republic (509–45 BCE)

The last king was thrown out of Rome in 509 BCE. The city was then governed by two elected consuls who were advised by the senate. Roman men attended an assembly where they voted on laws.

In 497 BCE Rome went to war with other Latin city-states and assumed power over them in a treaty undertaken in 493. In 390 the city was attacked by Celts from the north. Within a few years a wall was built around Rome's seven hills. By this time Rome had conquered all the surrounding city-states and was by far the biggest and most important city in Italy. Some of the people from other cities were allowed to become Roman citizens and vote in the assembly. In return they had to trade exclusively with Rome and provide soldiers for the Roman army.

The Punic Wars

Rome's desire to expand soon brought it into conflict with Carthage, a powerful North African city-state. Carthaginian commercial and military influence was strong throughout the Mediterranean, especially on the island of Sicily.

In 264 BCE Rome began a war with Carthage in Sicily. In 146 BCE, after three long wars (known as the Punic Wars), Carthage and its empire were finally destroyed. Rome had won the battle for the Mediterranean. Now the undoubted major power in the region, Rome could expand as it wished.

End of the Republic

From about 100 BCE there was increasing tension in Rome. A succession of consuls, including Sulla and Marius, became more powerful than consuls were intended to be. Their various ambitions to be absolute rulers of Rome violated the principles of the republic. Eventually the common people revolted, and civil war broke out. In 45 BCE, a powerful general named Julius Caesar took power for himself and ended the republican system of government. In 27 BCE Augustus established the imperial system of government and named himself emperor, sole ruler of the Roman world.

The Empire (27 BCE–476 CE)

Despite some disastrous emperors, the Roman Empire continued to expand across the Mediterranean. From 117 CE onward, a series of good emperors consolidated the empire and brought a period of stability to Rome. However, the third century CE was chaotic, with short reigns, unstable governments, and emperors frequently murdered

or overthrown. One emperor, Valerian, was captured by invading Persians and died in captivity. Diocletian tried to stabilize the empire, but his efforts led to civil war.

DIOCLETIAN C. 243–315 CE

Diocletian, one of the later Roman emperors, was probably the son of a freed slave. He rose to the level of military commander and was declared emperor by the army after the murder of the previous emperor in 284. He took over at a critical time. Invaders threatened all the empire's borders, and there were civil wars at home. Diocletian split the empire into east and west and had the idea of creating four emperors (tetrarchs), each taking responsibility for a certain area of the empire. He reorganized the provinces to get better control over them and began a program of building and defensive works to protect the empire's borders. He revised the taxes that citizens had to pay and brought in measures to control prices and wages. Although most of his ideas were good ones, they failed to restore the power of Rome. When he retired and declared himself a god in 305, civil war broke out between the emperors. Diocletian visited Rome only once in his life. After he died, his wife and son were executed by one of the emperors who replaced him.

◀ During the period of the republic, many quarrels arose in the Roman senate. This nineteenth-century fresco shows the senator Cicero revealing the plans of Catiline to lead an uprising against the senate in 63 BCE.

In 324 Constantine took power over the whole empire. Although he brought stability, Constantine realized that he could no longer protect the western part from invasion. He moved the empire's capital to Byzantium, which he renamed Constantinople (modern-day Istanbul, Turkey). After his death the empire again broke up and was invaded by many different tribes.

Rome itself was attacked in 410. The capital of the Western Roman Empire, however, had moved to Ravenna, on the east coast of Italy. Ravenna was invaded in 476, and with its fall the Roman Empire in the west came to an end, although the Eastern Roman Empire, whose capital was Constantinople, survived into the fifteenth century.

How the Empire Was Run

The imperial system (unlike the republican system) was hereditary, rule being passed from father to son. There were frequent clashes between emperor and senate, and successive emperors gradually reduced the power of the senate. Some emperors called assemblies very rarely.

The Roman provinces were run by governors assisted by the *equites*—middle-class Romans. The governor was a powerful figure, and several corrupt governors misused this power. The Roman economy depended on its provinces to provide its needs, including slaves, food, precious metals, cloth, wine, horses, and wild animals for the games. In return Rome offered its provinces peace and protection from invaders.

▶ *Emperor Constantine the Great reigned from 306 to 337 CE, becoming sole emperor in 324. Constantine reunited the Roman Empire, created the new capital city of Constantinople, and extended the rights of Christians within the empire.*

The Social Classes

Four-fifths of the empire's people worked on the land. In the countryside slaves on big farms owned by wealthy senators did most of the work. The produce was brought into the cities to sell. Poorer citizens had their own small piece of land on which they grew their own food.

About a million people lived in Rome itself. In the cities poor people served in shops, worked on building sites, or manufactured goods in workshops. Wealthier men owned small businesses, ran shops, or worked as civil servants. The very rich lived in great houses and had many slaves.

Because of the huge amount of cheap labor, very little labor-saving machinery was invented. Slaves came from all over the empire and by the end of the republic numbered about one million in Italy alone. Slaves served in all areas of Roman society, teaching the children of wealthy families, advising emperors, working in mines, and fighting in the games. A fortunate slave could save up enough money to buy his own freedom.

The City

Roman cities were grand places with great public temples, avenues, meeting places, and gardens. Rich people lived in big houses, often with gardens, their own water supply, and private toilets. They had cooks and servants to look after their needs. In colder climates they even had central heating systems, in which slaves fanned hot air through hollow walls in their houses. Poor people lived in buildings with no sanitation, open windows, and no heating or cooking facilities. They bought cooked food from stalls in the street. Very poor people in the city depended on handouts of bread from the rich.

▲ This second-century-CE Roman villa at Utica (in modern Tunisia, North Africa) is the only Roman villa still standing on African soil. Utica was the original capital of the Roman province of Africa.

THE ROMAN STATESMAN AND PHILOSOPHER SENECA (C. 4 BCE–65 CE) COMMENTS ON SLAVERY:

Remember that he whom you call slave came into life by the same route as you, basks in the same sky, and breathes, lives, and dies in the same way that you do. You can observe the free man in him just as he can see the slave in you. . . . You look down at your peril on someone in whose place you could come to be even while you look down on him.

SENECA, *EPISTLES*, XLVII

Every Roman city had at least one bathhouse where people of all classes might spend an afternoon lounging and enjoying hot, warm, and cold baths. At dusk people went to bed. At that time the streets became dangerous because heavy traffic was allowed into the city to deliver goods and food.

Women

Women were not considered Roman citizens. Girls were thought to belong to their father, and married women, to their husband. Until the later years of the republican era, women could not own property. Rich women ran their homes while poor women went out to work. Women worked in all areas of Roman life.

Children

Wealthy Roman children went to school until they were about twelve. Both boys and girls attended public schools. After the age of twelve, girls stayed at home and learned good housekeeping while boys stayed at school. At the age of fourteen, a girl got engaged, and at sixteen a boy became a citizen. Poor children worked alongside their parents.

Religion

At religious festivals, including weddings, the priests sacrificed animals to the gods and inspected the animals' organs to see if the gods approved. They believed that they could foretell the future by looking at the animals or by examining the sky for signs.

▼ *This marble relief carving from the tomb of a young child shows Roman children playing.*

When a wealthy man died, his body was carried in a procession outside of the city to be cremated. Musicians accompanied the funeral, and items were thrown into the cremation fire for use in the afterlife.

Culture

The most impressive Roman architecture incorporated arches and vaults (designs learned from the Etruscans) and tall columns (copied from the Greeks). The Romans also used concrete, their own invention. They constructed stone bridges and aqueducts for carrying water into cities. The walls of grand houses were decorated with paintings, and the floors with mosaics.

Among the best-known Roman literature are the poems of Catullus, Horace, and Virgil and the comic plays of Plautus. Other famous Roman authors wrote histories or books about the law and ethics. The favorite Roman entertainments were the chariot races held at the Circus Maximus and the games, where people watched slaves, criminals, and wild animals fight to the death.

The Legacy of Rome

Many of the world's legal and political systems are based on Roman models. Latin is the root of many of the world's most widely spoken languages. The Romans gave the world an enormous range of inventions, from the postal service and the fire brigade to newspapers, apartment blocks, calendars, concrete, and even flushing toilets.

SEE ALSO

- Augustus • Caesar, Julius • Caligula
- Claudius • Constantine • Hadrian
- Marcus Aurelius • Nero

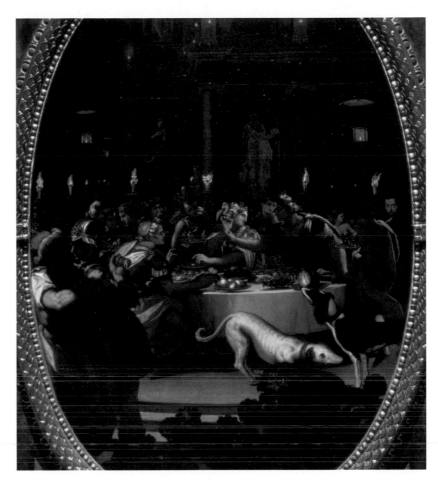

▲ This sixteenth century CE Italian watercolor shows a typically lavish Roman banquet attended by Cleopatra.

RICH ROMANS FREQUENTLY GAVE HUGE DINNER PARTIES WHERE THEIR GUESTS RECLINED IN ARMCHAIRS TO EAT THEIR FOOD WHILE POETS RECITED VERSE AND MUSICIANS PLAYED. SOMETIMES DINNER GUESTS WENT TO A SPECIAL ROOM TO VOMIT SO THAT THEY COULD GO ON EATING EVEN AFTER THEY WERE FULL. THE WRITER MARTIAL (C. 40–C. 103 CE) DESCRIBES SOME OF THE DELICACIES TO BE FOUND ON A DINNER PARTY MENU:

Mallow leaves (good for digestion) . . . lettuce, chopped leeks, mint (for burping), rocket leaves . . . mackerel garnished with rue and sliced egg, and a sow's udder marinated in tuna fish brine . . . that's the hors d'oeuvres. For the main course, all served together, tender cuts of lamb, with beans and spring greens, and a chicken and a ham left over from three previous dinners. When you are full, fresh fruit and vintage wine . . .

MARTIAL, EPIGRAMS X. 48, 7–19

Rome, City of

Rome, the city at the heart of the Roman world, lies in the valley of the Tiber River, twelve miles (20 km) inland from the western coast of central Italy. Long before people settled the region, the Tiber had carved out a landscape of low hills rising from the plain. It was on this high ground that Rome was built.

Rome's Legendary Origins

Ancient Romans told two stories about the origins of their mother city. In one, Aeneas, a Trojan warrior, fled from his eastern homeland. After much wandering his journey ended in present-day Italy. Aeneas married a king's daughter, and their descendants built Rome.

In another myth, the Romans told how the twins Romulus and Remus were thrown into the Tiber. They were found by a she-wolf, who suckled them, and they were later raised by a shepherd. The boys grew into strong young men and built a city on the banks of the river. Unable to decide who should be king or what to call the city, they fought. Romulus killed Remus, and he built a city that he named Rome, after himself. The city was supposedly founded in 753 BCE.

The True Origin of Rome

Archaeologists date Rome's origin to around 1000 BCE, when settlers built villages on the summits of the area's hills, near a ford in the river. By around 750 BCE these farming communities had merged into a town. During the 600s BCE, the marshy valley at the foothills was drained, and the Forum Romanum (Roman forum) was laid

▶ This model shows part of Rome as it may have looked during the early fourth century CE. This view looks west from the Palatine Hill toward the Tiber River. The largest building in the foreground is the Temple of Venus Felix and Roma Aeterna.

out. During the 500s, fortifications were built to protect the town, temples were constructed, and the first bridge was erected over the Tiber.

This initial phase of expansion happened during the monarchic era, when the city was ruled by Etruscan kings. Rome emerged as one of the largest cities of the Mediterranean. In 509 BCE the last of these foreign rulers was overthrown. From then on Rome was ruled by its leading citizens, and the Roman Republic began.

Republican Rome

At the center of republican Rome was the Roman forum, a narrow rectangular space used for commercial, political, religious, and social activities. At first shops and houses surrounded it, but they were moved away as the forum's ceremonial activities became more important. Houses for aristocrats were situated on the Palatine Hill, while the poor settled in Rome's overcrowded suburbs. During the second century BCE temples were built around the forum, as were basilicas for government offices and law courts. Aqueducts brought in fresh water, paved roads crossed the city, and the first stone theater was built.

The Roman Empire

The Roman Republic ended in 27 BCE, and a new period in Rome's history began. From 27 BCE until 476 CE, Rome was ruled by emperors. Rome's first emperor, Augustus (reigned 27 BCE–14 CE), boasted that he had transformed Rome from a brick city to one of marble.

▼ *Imperial Rome in about 300 CE.*

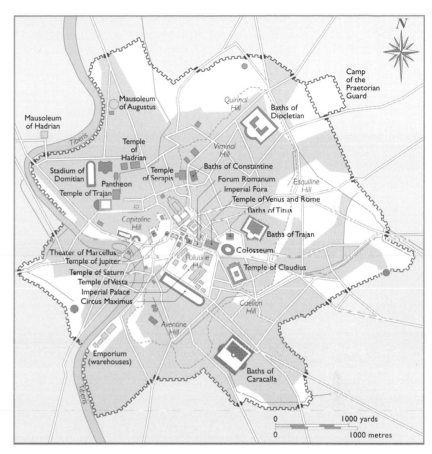

THE PANTHEON

Built between 118 and 126 CE to replace a smaller temple on the same site, the Pantheon is a masterpiece of Roman architecture. It was built as a temple for the twelve Olympian gods, hence the name Pantheon ("all gods"). Its great dome is made of concrete and measures 146 feet (44.4 m) from floor to ceiling. At the top of the dome is an oculus (eye) twenty-nine feet (8.8 m) across, through which daylight enters the building. As the oculus is not covered, the floor is slightly concave and has a drain at its center to catch rain that falls through.

I completed the Forum Julium and the basilica that is between the temple of Castor and the temple of Saturn . . . and when the same basilica was burned down, I began to rebuild it on a larger site. . . . I repaired eighty-two temples of the gods in the city . . . rebuilt the via Flaminia . . . and all the bridges between the Milvian and the Minucian.

AUGUSTUS, *RES GESTAE*

▼ Beyond the ruins of the Roman forum, the Arch of Titus, built in 81 CE by Domitian to commemorate the taking of Jerusalem, still stands.

Augustus built temples, basilicas, theaters, baths, libraries, aqueducts, and a new forum (the forum of Augustus). Emperors after Augustus also left their mark on the city: the Colosseum was started by Vespasian (reigned 69–79 CE) and completed by Titus (reigned 79–81); Trajan (reigned 98–117) created a market and a column that commemorated his battle victories; Hadrian (reigned 117–138) erected the Pantheon; and Caracalla (reigned 211–217) added a complex of baths. All of these constructions survive in present-day Rome.

Rome after 300 CE

In the early 300s CE, when Rome had a population of one and a half million, a list of its buildings was drawn up. There were 28 libraries, 8 bridges, 11 town squares, 10 basilicas, 19 aqueducts, 1,352 drinking fountains, 11 big bathhouses, 856 small bathhouses, 29 main roads, 2 racetracks, 2 amphitheaters, 3 theaters, 36 triumphal arches, 37 gateways through the city wall, 290 warehouses, 254 corn mills, 1,797 houses of the rich, 46,602 apartments and small houses, and 144 public lavatories.

Constantine I (reigned 306–337 CE) moved the capital of the Roman Empire to the new city of Constantinople (present-day Istanbul). As a result, Rome was neglected, and its position gravely weakened. In 410 CE the city was sacked by barbarian invaders. Thereafter, as the empire in the west collapsed, Rome's magnificent buildings gradually fell into ruin.

SEE ALSO

• Aeneid • Architecture • Augustus
• Hadrian • Roman Mythology
• Roman Republic and Empire

Sacrifices

Sacrifice, the act of offering something to a god—food, animals, clothing, incense, or even people—was part of the religious practice of many ancient societies. People offered sacrifices to obtain favors or blessings, to atone for wrongdoing, and to ward off disaster.

The earliest form of sacrifice in the world was practiced in the Upper Paleolithic age (c. 35,000–13,500 BCE.) Hunters would bury a young reindeer or cast its body into a lake to secure a bountiful hunting season. Hunters also buried possessions or threw them in the lake along with a doe as proof of their willingness to suffer. Sometimes they hung an older reindeer's skull and antlers on a pole to mark the earliest-known sacrificial altars.

Human Sacrifice

Early agricultural societies believed the gods controlled the fertility of the earth. To ensure a good harvest, they offered the gods the essence of life itself: human blood. Victims were generally tied to an altar, stabbed to death with a sacrificial knife, and then burned. Fire played a part in the sacrifice rituals of many societies, because of the belief that offerings were conveyed to the gods via the smoke rising from the altar.

In northern and western Europe ancient Celts killed people in sacrifice rituals and buried them in bogs—heavily waterlogged patches of earth. Because bogs have low temperatures and are low in oxygen and rich in tannic acid, the bodies of several sacrifice victims have been found naturally preserved.

Babylonians pushed their victims—slaves, criminals, and children—off the edges of ziggurats (pyramid-shaped temples). There is widespread evidence of human sacrifices in the Moche culture, which flourished on the northern coast of present-day Peru between about 200 and 800 CE. Moche ceramics have scenes of ritual sacrifrices, and archaeologists have found skeletons of sacrificed people with their neckbone cut or broken.

▼ This detail from a Celtic cauldron made and used in the first century CE shows people being sacrificed to Teutates, the god of war and wealth, who was worshiped mostly in Gaul (present-day France).

Roman law forbade human sacrifice. Yet the gladiatorial games, in both republican and imperial times, were bloody events ending in the death of most of the participants, largely to appease the violent tastes of the mob. Nevertheless, the Romans drew the line at killing people in the name of the gods: they considered it barbaric. The Romans viewed the rites of the Druids (Celtic priests) with abhorrence and accused them of murdering children.

Animal Sacrifice

By the end of the second millennium BCE, human sacrifice was on the wane in many places. As civilization developed and grew more sophisticated, people tended to place a higher value on human life. Animals were sacrificed instead, their blood poured into bowls and offered to the gods.

The Greeks sacrificed many domesticated animals. They hoped the offerings would please the gods, who would then favor them with good harvests, health, and fortune. Sacrifice was also thought to purify a place. Greeks would sacrifice an animal in order to cleanse an area of evil and make it habitable for the gods. Sacrifices were offered at oracles, during festivals, and at ceremonies initiating people into secret religious societies. Animals sacrificed were often associated with the god being worshiped. Horses were offered to Helios, the sun god thought to travel across the heavens in a chariot. Pregnant sows were sacrificed in honor of Demeter, the goddess of the earth. Valuable bulls were sacrificed to Zeus, one of whose symbols was a bull.

Crop Sacrifice

The Romans sacrificed animals and vegetables. Before sowing their crops, Roman farmers killed a sow in honor of Ceres, the goddess of nature. Harvest cakes were also offered to Jupiter, the god of the sky, who was believed to send rain. The Romans also offered milk, wine, oil, and honey. The tradition of sacrificing the fruits of the harvest dates back to prehistory, when people started raising crops in western Asia.

▶ *This Greek vase, made sometime between 480 and 490 BCE, shows the gods Apollo and Artemis worshiping at the altar of Zeus, the chief god. Apollo plays music on his lyre, while Artemis pours an offering into the fire.*

The Romans thought of wine as the blood of the grape and as the lifeblood of the earth itself. It was offered to the gods and also, together with water, sacrificed in honor of the dead as a symbol of life.

In a festival called Shavuot, ancient Jews took the first fruits of their orchard to the temple in Jerusalem. Hindus left grains, fruits, and flowers on their altars to thank the gods.

Sacrificers

In most communities the sacrificer was the head of a family, a clan, or a tribe. In many civilizations kings conducted important sacrifices. In Egypt the pharaoh, who was also the high priest, took part in elaborate sacrificial ceremonies during which he was thought to be communicating with the gods. Babylonian kings offered cattle sacrifices to the god Marduk during Akidu, the New Year festival. On less important occasions, sacrifices were conducted by priests, usually on altars outside the temple. After being slaughtered and burned, the animals were then eaten. In Rome and Greece people also offered sacrifices at home or at roadside altars.

▲ *This scene, part of a marble monument erected by a Roman consul named Cnaeus Domitius Ahenobarbus around 100 BCE, shows a procession of people preparing to make an animal sacrifice to Mars, the god of war.*

A FARMER IN ANCIENT ROME OFFERS SACRIFICE TO JANUS, A GOD OF THE HARVEST:

Father Janus, in offering these cakes to you, I humbly pray that you will be merciful to me and my children, my house and my household.

CATO THE ELDER, *THE PLANTING RITUAL* (C. 160 BCE)

Christian Sacrifice

In the first century CE, the early Christians introduced a new conception of sacrifice. They interpreted Jesus' death on the cross as God's sacrifice of his son in order to cleanse mankind of sin. Since then this ultimate sacrifice has been remembered in the Eucharist—the most important ceremony in the religious life of Christians.

SEE ALSO

- Babylonians • Death and Burial • Festivals
- Mummification • Religion • Tombs

Samudra Gupta

Samudra Gupta (died c. 380 CE) was the second ruler of the Gupta dynasty. When he inherited the throne in about 335 from his father, Chandra Gupta I, the Guptas ruled only the valley of the Ganges River in northeastern India. Samudra Gupta added vast territories to his Indian empire, conquering most of southeastern India and kingdoms to the north as far as the Himalayas.

Samudra Gupta ruled over the northern kingdoms directly, but he allowed local southern rulers to remain on their throne in return for their acclaim and their recognition of his sovereignty. Samudra Gupta ruled his empire for more than forty years. After his death his sons, Rama Gupta and Chandra Gupta II, each ruled the empire in turn.

Coins

Samudra Gupta was the first of the Guptas to mint coins. They were made of gold and usually decorated with royal portraits and images of the Hindu god Vishnu or his consort Lakshmi. Some coins also depict Garuda, the sacred eagle who carried Vishnu across the skies. Although Samudra Gupta favored Vishnu especially, he was tolerant of all religions. For instance, he let the king of Lanka build Buddhist monasteries within his Hindu empire.

That one of Samudra Gupta's coin portraits displays him playing a *veena*, a stringed instrument similar to a harp, suggests that he wanted to be seen as a patron of the arts as well as a warrior. His court was filled with scholars and writers, such as the poet Harishena, whose job was to compose verses praising the king.

▶ Samudra Gupta was inspired by the coins of the earlier Kushan Empire (c. 100–240 CE), which were still circulating in northern India. On this gold coin, the king plays an instrument called a veena.

THE FOLLOWING VERSES IN PRAISE OF SAMUDRA GUPTA WERE WRITTEN BY THE POET HARISHENA AND CARVED ON THE COLUMN AT ALLAHABAD:

This high column proclaims the fame of the glorious Samudra Gupta . . .

Who was skillful in fighting a hundred battles . . .

Whose most charming body was covered over with the beautiful marks of a hundred battle wounds . . .

Who made all the kings of the forest countries his servants . . .

Who rubbed out the fame of other kings with the soles of his feet . . .

Whose fame fills the whole world . . .

Who, being full of compassion, had a tender heart . . .

Who was the giver of many hundreds of thousands of cows . . .

Who was a mortal only in celebrating the rites of mankind,

But in other respects a god dwelling on the earth.

HARISHENA (LATE FOURTH CENTURY CE)

Inscriptions on Stone

Two sets of verses praising Samudra Gupta are extant, both inscribed on stone. One is carved on a rock at Eran in central India, while the other is on a column in the north at Allahabad. These verses list his victories and praise him in lavish terms. "His very mighty fame is always circling round about," says the Eran inscription, "His enemies are terrified . . . even in the intervals of dreaming [of him]."

Almost all that is known about Samudra Gupta comes from his coins and these rock inscriptions. Thus, historians know only what the king wanted them to know about him. The peoples he conquered probably had a very different view of Samudra Gupta.

SEE ALSO

• Buddhism • Gupta Empire • Hinduism
• Pataliputra

◄ *Much of what is known of Samudra Gupta's reign comes from the inscription on this column in Allahabad, India.*

Sanchi

One of the most spectacular archaeological sites in India is Sanchi, a hilltop Buddhist monastery complex in Madhya Pradesh. Founded by the Mauryan emperor Ashoka in the third century BCE, the monastery contains around fifty monuments within a small area.

The monuments of Sanchi, which include temples, pillars, sculptures, and dome-shaped structures called stupas, date from the third century BCE to the twelfth century CE. This latter date coincides with the disappearance of Buddhism from its Indian homeland, although by then the religion had been in decline for a long time. The Sanchi monuments thus represent almost the entire development of Indian Buddhist art and architecture, covering a period of around 1,400 years.

Ashoka's Great Stupa at Sanchi

When he founded Sanchi, the Mauryan emperor Ashoka set up a stupa and a polished stone pillar, which he topped with four carved lions inscribed with royal edicts (announcements).

Builders subsequently enlarged Ashoka's stupa until it was 120 feet (37 m) across and 54 feet (16.5 m) high, not counting its spire. They added a raised walkway, stairs, and four elaborately carved stone *toranas* (gateways). These gateways date from the first century BCE and are considered the most beautiful works of art in Sanchi. The gateways are covered with reliefs showing animals, birds, gods, goddesses, and scenes from the Buddha's life. When these *toranas* were made, the Buddha was not shown in human form. Instead, he was represented by a throne, a wheel, a bo tree, footprints, or a stupa.

▼ *On the eastern gateway of the Great Stupa at Sanchi, carved elephants on top of the sandstone columns support richly decorated architraves (cross beams).*

WHAT IS A STUPA?

▼ On the north gateway of the Great Stupa, horses and riders fill the spaces between the architraves.

Stupa is a Sanskrit word that means "topknot" (of hair) or "summit." Originally burial mounds, stupas were later designed to hold sacred relics, such as bones, or the belongings of the Buddha and other holy men. In India, as in medieval Europe, relics were believed to radiate power. Worshipers could access this power by walking clockwise around the stupa. The Great Stupa at Sanchi has two walkways for this purpose, one at ground level and the other a third of the way up.

There are various theories about the religious design of stupas. A stupa's mound may represent the dome of the sky or a sacred mountain linking heaven and earth. Decorated with three parasols (sunshades), the spire on top may stand for the "three jewels" of Buddhism: the Buddha, the dharma (the law), and the Sangha (the order of monks). Another idea is that it is there to protect the relics, as a parasol protects its holder from the sun.

Stupas were built not by monks but by kings, nobles, and merchants. Rich merchants from the neighboring city, Vidisha, paid for many of the stupas at Sanchi. Constructing a stupa was their way to gain religious merit without becoming a monk. According to Buddhist belief, 84,000 stupas were built during Ashoka's reign in India.

The western gateway is covered with wicked grinning demons who are trying to distract Buddha because they want to stop him from reaching enlightenment. The northern gateway shows him performing the miracle of walking through the air. On the eastern gateway, animals and gods pay their respects to the empty throne, representing the enlightened Buddha. A king, who may be Ashoka himself, appears on the southern gateway, where he is shown visiting a stupa with his court.

SEE ALSO
• Ashoka
• Buddhism
• Mauryan Empire

Sappho

Though Sappho is one of only a few female poets of ancient Greece, she is considered one of its great poets. She lived in the late seventh century BCE, and spent most of her life on the island of Lesbos. It is difficult to be certain about many details of Sappho's life, as they were recorded in biographies written long after she died.

Biographers claim that Sappho came from a wealthy family and had three brothers, one of whom was a successful wine merchant in Egypt. Later she married a prosperous merchant and had a daughter, Cleis, whom she describes in a poem as "a beautiful child, golden like flowers, for whom I would not take the whole of Lydia."

▼ This marble sculpture of Sappho, dating from the nineteenth century, shows the poet in contemplative mood, her lyre beside her.

Sappho's Reputation

Sappho was a subject of fascination in ancient Greece. One story relates how she threw herself off the cliffs of Levkas because a man she loved did not love her in return. Playwrights portrayed her as unattractive, small, and masculine, without ever having seen her.

Sappho was also honored in ancient Greece. A coin bearing her image was minted in Lesbos. Hearing one of her songs, the Athenian ruler Solon is supposed to have said that he "wanted to learn it and die." A statue of Sappho was erected in Syracuse, a Greek colony in Sicily where her relatives lived for a while.

Sappho's Group

Sappho's fame drew female poets to Lesbos. Her followers established an informal *hetaireia*, or group. Some of Sappho's poem's appear to be written to be sung at weddings. However, it is most likely that she and her friends performed them only in private settings. It is thought that Sappho was the leader of a school in Lesbos, where young aristocratic women came to learn to compose and sing poetry and perform on the lyre. Some sources claim these women also studied elegant behavior, charm, and dress to enhance their appeal as future wives.

Sappho's circle was essentially a close group of female poets who wrote and sang for their own artistic pleasure or at social events and religious occasions. As Sappho's poems reveal, the group was bonded by intense friendships.

Sappho's Originality

It is thought that Sappho invented the plectrum, a pick used to pluck the strings of a lyre. She was most original, however, in her way of writing about daily experiences, such as a picnic in an orchard or cattle coming home, using the word *I* more personally than other poets had done. She communicated intense feelings about ordinary concerns: children, gossip, love, and friendship.

Poetry in Fragments

Sappho's poetry has been retrieved in pieces. Fragments were discovered as late as the nineteenth century. Some papyri with poems had been reused as mummy cloth, but most fragments found had been thrown on garbage dumps in ancient Egypt. Ancient biographers claim she wrote nine books, but only one poem survives complete. In it she asks Aphrodite, goddess of love, to help her to win the love of a girl.

▶ *Of the two lyre players on this ancient Greek vase, the female figure on the left is thought to be Sappho.*

SEE ALSO

• Festivals • Greece, Classical • Literature
• Music and Dance • Women • Writing

THIS IS A FRAGMENT OF A POEM ADDRESSED TO THE EVENING STAR, HESPERUS. A BRIDE WENT FROM HER MOTHER'S HOME TO HER NEW HUSBAND'S IN THE EVENING:

Hesperus, loveliest of all the stars . . .
bringing back all that glowing Dawn sent forth:
you bring the sheep,
you bring the goat,
you bring the girl to a home away from her mother.

SAPPHO

Sargon of Akkad

Sargon reigned as king of Mesopotamia for fifty years from about 2334 BCE. He unified Sumerian territory and established a new royal capital at the city of Akkad. As few texts written during his lifetime survive, knowledge of Sargon and his achievements is for the most part based on legendary accounts. His reputation became so great that stories about him were recorded by scribes for centuries after his death.

▼ This Akkadian head, crafted in bronze from a cast, was made between 2334 and 2154 BCE and is believed to represent Sargon of Akkad.

Archaeologists have not located Akkad, but it is thought to have been in central Mesopotamia, near present-day Baghdad, Iraq. As the Akkadian kingdom included several different regions and ethnic groups, historians consider Sargon to be the ruler of the world's first empire. In Mesopotamian writings, he is heralded as a great king who conquered other cities and lands.

Sargon's Empire

During Sargon's reign, ships from the Indus region and from lands bordering the Persian Gulf visited Akkad. The city may have established commercial links with the Mediterranean.

Sargon was the first Mesopotamian ruler to establish a professsional army; he claimed to have fought over thirty battles and to have had "5,400 men eat daily before him." His first victory was over the city of Erech (Uruk). At the height of Sargon's reign, his territory encompassed all of Mesopotamia as well as the land of the Elamites, and it reached north into present-day Syria.

Stories of Sargon

In one well-known story about Sargon, some merchants requested the king's assistance in a local dispute in present-day central Turkey. The legend claims Sargon traveled there with a group of warriors to settle the quarrel, crossing many mountains and rivers on the way. Generations of Mesopotamians who lived after Sargon regarded him as the founder of a military tradition of which they felt proud.

The various Mesopotamian texts that refer to Sargon say little about his personal history. His mother was a priestess, his father is unknown, and he rose to become a cupbearer to a king of Kish, a Sumerian city. The story of Sargon's birth and miraculous survival as a child, which bears some resemblance to the biblical story of Moses, is probably a myth.

At Ur, Sargon installed his daughter Enheduanna as priestess of the moon god Nanna-Suen. The Sumerian hymns she composed have survived, and thus she is the world's first known female author.

▶ *Found in Susa, at the mouth of the Euphrates River in present-day Iran, this Akkadian carving from around 2350 BCE shows enemies of the Akkadians caught in a net.*

SEE ALSO

• Akkadians • Elamites • Ishtar
• Mesopotamia

Sasanians

The Sasanian kings ruled what is now Iran from 224 to 636 CE. The dynasty took its name from Sasan, grandfather of the first Sasanian king, Ardashir. The Sasanians set out to restore the glories of the earlier Achaemenid kings of Persia. They promoted the ancient religion of Zoroastrianism and strove to reconquer all the provinces that had been Persian when Cyrus the Great and Darius ruled.

The Sasanian kings ordered the destruction of all records and inscriptions from the period when Persia had been ruled by the "foreign" Parthian kings. The first Sasanian king, Ardashir, even changed his name to Artaxerxes to remind his subjects of the link between the old and new Persian kingdoms.

A State Religion

The Sasanian kings ruled different peoples who worshiped their own gods. Shapur I was a particularly tolerant king who allowed his subjects to worship as they pleased. He even met the prophet Manichaeus (or Mani), who preached his own unconventional form of Christianity at Shapur's court. However, the later Sasanian kings permitted only Zoroastrianism, the official state religion. Manichaeus was arrested and executed in 276 by King Varahram (or Bahram) II. This act sparked a series of persecutions in which other faiths, including Christianity and Judaism, were outlawed and their followers harshly treated. The power of the *mobad*, or high priest, of Zoroastrianism grew steadily. By 350 CE, along with religion, the *mobad* had great influence in such areas of Persian life as the law, trade, and government.

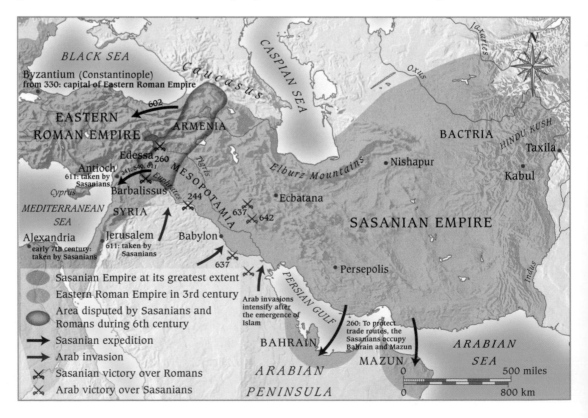

► *Sasanian Persia between 224 and 642 CE.*

ENEMIES OF ROME

The Sasanian kings were determined to push the Romans out of western Asia. In the years after 245 CE, Shapur I (reigned 241–272 CE) forced the Roman army to retreat from Mesopotamia and Armenia. In a second campaign in the 250s, he sacked many of the rich Roman cities in Syria and Asia Minor. Thousands of Roman captives were forcibly deported and resettled in distant provinces of the Sasanian Empire.

Rome struggled to deal with this powerful new force on its eastern frontier. The emperor Gordian III was mysteriously assassinated in Mesopotamia just as he was preparing to attack. Philippus I had to buy peace with the Sasanians by offering them gifts of gold and silver. At Edessa in 260, the Romans suffered one of their greatest disasters when the emperor Valerian was captured and murdered. Shapur ordered the carving of monumental scenes showing the Roman emperor as his helpless prisoner.

The Romans had few victories against the Sasanian Empire until Julian marched his army into Mesopotamia in the middle of the fourth century.

▶ This Persian miniature from the 14th century CE shows the first Sasanian king, Ardashir (also known as Artaxerxes), ordering the execution of Ardavan (Artabanus), the last Parthian king, in 224 CE.

SASANIANS

224 CE
Ardashir Papakan revolts against Parthian overlords.

238 CE
Ardashir campaigns against Roman Mesopotamia.

245 CE
Shapur I captures Roman outposts in Mesopotamia.

260 CE
Sasanians capture and kill the Roman emperor Valerian at Edessa.

348 CE
King Shapur II defeats Emperor Constantius II.

428 CE
Armenia is recaptured from Rome by Varahram (Bahram) V.

531 CE
The greatest Sasanian king, Chosroes I, comes to the throne.

615 CE
Sasanian Empire is at its height under Chosroes II.

623 CE
Invasion of Sasanian Empire by the Byzantine emperor Heraclius.

636 CE
Sasanians are ousted from Mesopotamia by Islamic Arabs.

651 CE
Persia is overrun by Islamic Arabs; Yazdagird III flees to India.

CHOSROES I *REIGNED 531–579 CE*

Chosroes I became king at a time when Iran had been weakened by feeble kings. The kingdom was poorly defended, warring nobles were ignoring the king's authority, and White Huns and Turks of central Asia threatened to invade Iran's northern frontiers.

Chosroes set up a new system of tax collection, and with the extra money raised, he built a powerful army run by his loyal generals rather than by old noble families. He captured the rich trading city of Antioch in 540. He crushed the White Hun invaders in 558 and fought a twenty-year war against the Eastern Roman Empire.

Chosroes was not only a warrior; he built the beautiful arch at Ctesiphon, which was celebrated for centuries as the world's largest vaulted building. To encourage learning and the arts, Chosroes established schools, libraries, and temples. Old roads, canals, and aqueducts were restored to working order. He encouraged an interest in farming, crafts, and science. As a result of his accomplishments, Chosroes's long reign was remembered as a golden age.

The Coming of Islam

In the early seventh century, the Sasanian kings made a great effort to capture those parts of Asia that were still under Roman control. They fought the Eastern Roman Empire and captured Antioch, Jerusalem, and Alexandria in Egypt.

In 628 Iranian troops besieged the eastern Roman capital of Constantinople. In return the Roman emperor Heraclius marched against Persia and captured the Sasanian royal palace near Ctesiphon in Mesopotamia. As a result of these long wars, the regime was exhausted just as a new invader appeared on its borders.

In the 630s and early 640s, Arab armies conquered Persia and brought their new Islamic faith. The army of the last Sasanian king, Yazdagird III, was destroyed by the Arabs in 637. Yazdagird fled to his lands in the east but was eventually murdered. With his death the Sasanian kingdom came to an end, and its territory became a part of the Arab-ruled Islamic Empire.

◀ *This silver dish shows an unknown Sasanian king sitting within a pavilion flanked by two guards. The dish, which probably dates from the sixth century CE, is in a native Persian style with little trace of earlier Greek and Parthian influences.*

SEE ALSO

- Achaemenids • Alexandria • Huns
- Parthians • Zoroastrianism

Science

Science is a field of knowledge encompassing the natural world. Scientists study objects and events and draw up theories and rules about the way things work. Modern science has dozens of different branches. In ancient times, however, science did not exist as a separate discipline; knowledge of the world was simply part of everyday life. Explanations for natural phenomena were often drawn from religious, magical, or philosophical knowledge.

What modern historians know about ancient science comes mainly from the records and artifacts of a small number of civilizations. These civilizations had written languages in which they could record their scientific endeavors.

Materials

People discovered how to create, form, and use different materials through chance, curiosity, and experimentation. Early experiments in combining substances produced the first paints and dyes from crushed berries and rocks mixed with a little water.

Pottery seems to have arisen from the discovery that clay can be easily shaped when it is wet and that it hardens into a highly useful material when left to dry in the sun. The metalworking of copper and bronze is believed to have started over five thousand years ago. Around 2000 BCE, glass was first manufactured. The earliest glass objects were beads and seals made in western Asia. By 1400 BCE the ancient Egyptians had improved glassmaking to create jars, vessels, and perfume bottles. The Romans were expert builders, and around 200 BCE they learned how to mix cement with other materials to form a valuable building material called concrete.

The Egyptians made the first paper from papyrus reeds as early as 3000 BCE. Around 100 CE the Chinese made paper from pulped silk waste. Later, bark, bamboo, and hemp were used.

◄ By the fourteenth century BCE Egyptian glass making had become sufficiently advanced for the manufacture of such beautiful objects as this glass vase.

Medicine

The theory and practice of early medicine owed much to magic and religion. Nevertheless, many ancient civilizations made great strides in understanding the human body and treating injury and illness.

From the large numbers of medical papyri, it is known that the ancient Egyptians had a very good understanding of the human body and internal organs, knew the difference between many different diseases, and knew about the importance of healthy teeth and gums. They were one of the first cultures to perform surgical operations, such as lancing boils. They also learned how to set broken bones.

Ancient Chinese medicine used a selection of different natural compounds to treat a range of health problems. The Chinese also developed acupuncture, in which parts of the body are pricked with small needles. This practice is believed to heal the body by releasing blocked paths of energy. In Europe medicine continued to advance with the ancient Greeks and Romans, the latter shaping artificial limbs and performing simple eye operations to remove cataracts.

Mathematics

Egyptian number hieroglyphs dating to 3250 BCE have been found, and there is evidence that Babylonians were recording mathematical calculations around the same time. Whereas the decimal system, based on the number ten, is standard in the modern world, the Babylonian system was based on the number sixty. The Babylonians studied many areas of mathematics, including areas and volumes, and they knew how to perform complex multiplication and division.

The ancient Egyptians were the first to develop theories in the field of geometry—the mathematics of shapes—which they applied in the construction of large structures, including their pyramids. The ancient Greeks made great progress in geometry and other areas of mathematics. Great mathematicians, including Archimedes, Euclid, and Pythagoras, devised and proved theories that are still taught. In the Americas the Maya developed sophisticated calendars and a counting system based on the number twenty.

▼ A marble bust of the ancient Greek physician Hippocrates (c. 460– c. 375 BCE), who wrote many medical works on health, sanitation, and disease and who is considered the founder of medical science.

THE DISCOVERIES OF ARCHIMEDES

Archimedes (c. 287–212 BCE) lived in Syracuse on the eastern coast of Sicily. Although some remnants of his original works remain, most of what is known about his life and work comes from the Roman biographer Plutarch.

Archimedes was a brilliant mathematician. Among his many discoveries were an early approximation of the value of pi, a method for calculating the volume of spheres and cylinders, and an innovative way of expressing enormous numbers.

Although Archimedes believed that pure mathematics was the only worthy pursuit, much of his work was outside pure mathematics. He is said to have invented a simple pump for drawing water, called Archimedes' screw, that is still in use. His most famous mathematical achievement is called the Archimedes principle, which provides a method for calculating the volume of irregular shapes by placing them in water and measuring the volume of water displaced.

Archimedes also made important discoveries about levers. Levers pivot around one point called a fulcrum. The effort one applies on one side of the fulcrum can move a load on the other side. Archimedes found that the load one can move with a set amount of effort depended exactly on the distance of the load from the fulcrum and the effort.

While Syracuse was under siege by Roman forces, Archimedes is reputed to have developed war machines, including a giant crane and claw for turning ships upside down and a series of mirrors and lenses that focused the sun's rays onto one point to set materials alight. Despite these efforts, Syracuse fell, and Archimedes was killed by a Roman soldier.

▶ This tablet from ancient Babylon contains astronomical information for calculating the movement of the planet Jupiter.

The earliest example of the decimal number system is found in China around 1300 BCE. The Chinese were the first to use negative numbers. Then around 1 CE, the Chinese mathematician Liu Hsin used decimal fractions. The concept of zero, a number representing the absence of a value, came much later. It developed gradually in China and Mesopotamia from about 500 BCE.

Astronomy

Since long before history was written down, people have gazed at the night skies, searching for patterns and meaning. Through careful observation of the position and movement of the stars, many ancient civilizations were able to measure the changing of the seasons and construct accurate annual calendars.

Around 3000 BCE the Chinese were using a calendar of 365 days. Using the cycles of the moon, the ancient Egyptians also divided the year into 365 days, collected into 12 months of 30 days each. The 5 remaining days were regarded as the birthdays of the gods and set aside for festivals. Almost five thousand years ago, the ancient Babylonians were predicting with accuracy when eclipses of the moon would occur. The ancient Chinese were the first civilization to record a comet sighting, and further milestones in astronomy were reached by the ancient Greeks. One Greek astronomer, Hipparchus (second century BCE), constructed a catalog of 850 stars; invented the concept of a star's brightness, known as magnitude; and made some very precise measurements of star positions with only the naked eye.

Geography

As water and land transport developed, ancient peoples were able to journey long distances, and thus more was learned about the planet and how to travel around it.

Early astronomy provided a star guide with which to navigate on seas by night, and detailed mapmaking was practiced by many cultures, even those without a written language.

A simple map carved onto a mammoth tusk, perhaps dating to 12,000 BCE, has been found in present-day Ukraine. The earliest known map of a definite region is around 4,300 years old and shows part of the state of Akkad in Mesopotamia (present-day Iraq). It was produced by the Babylonians, who also were the first people to divide a circle into 360 equal parts, or degrees.

The ancient Greeks developed the notion of a grid of lines running vertically (longitude) and horizontally (latitude) around the earth to provide a system of plotting and measuring distance on a map. In China a brilliant scientist named Chang Heng developed a similar grid; according to his reasoning the earth was not flat but spherical. Around 130 CE Chang Heng also invented a simple version of a seismograph, a device that measures earth tremors and earthquakes.

▶ *This elaborately illustrated page from Pliny's* Historia Naturalis *comes from an Italian manuscript of the fifteenth century CE.*

SEE ALSO

PLINY THE ELDER 23–79 CE

Gaius Plinius Cecilius Secundus, known as Pliny the Elder, was a Roman scholar. He served in the military for twelve years and then as an official in various public positions. Pliny wrote at least seventy books on many different topics, but his most famous work was the *Historia Naturalis,* published in 77 CE. Consisting of thirty-seven separate volumes that together documented everything the Romans knew about science and the natural world, it is regarded as the first detailed scientific encyclopedia.

Pliny's scientific curiosity proved to be his undoing. Commanding a fleet of ships, he learned of the eruption of Mount Vesuvius. He went ashore to investigate and to help others, but he was overcome by fumes and died.

Scythians

The Scythians were not one people but a group of nomadic tribes who lived on the plains of central Asia. By 650 BCE they had moved to the territory that came to be known as Scythia, land lying between the Danube River in the west and the Don River in the east. The northern border of Scythia ran along the boundary between the grass steppes (plains) of the Ukraine and the thick forests of northern Russia. The southern boundary was the curving northern rim of the Black Sea.

The Scythians spoke an Indo-Iranian language but had no system of writing. Knowledge of them comes from Assyrian royal inscriptions and Persian records, in which they are named the Saka; from Greek writers, who named them Skythai; and from recent archaeological work in the region of their homeland.

Herodotus described the different tribes that lived in Scythia. The Alizones and Neuri, for example, were farming people who grew crops such as grain and millet. Greeks from the shores of the Black Sea traded and even intermarried with these settled tribes. Farther east the Scythian tribes were more warlike and probably enslaved the native populations to grow their food. The most powerful group were the proud and aristocratic Royal Scythians, who lived in the southern Crimea.

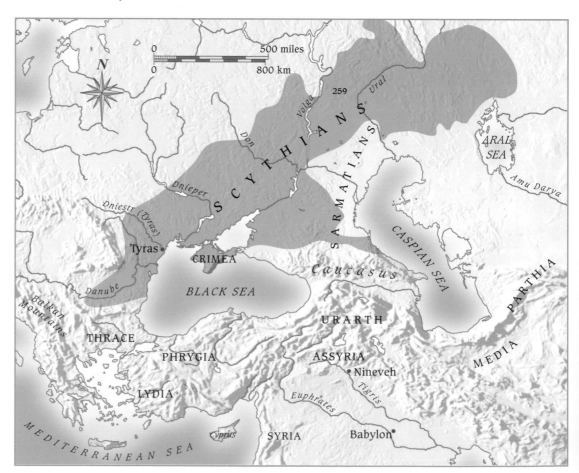

▶ The area inhabited by the Scythians around 400 BCE.

SCYTHIANS

c. 1500–1000 BCE

Scythians move from Volga-Ural steppes into the area north of the Black Sea.

c. 600 BCE

Persian records begin to mention the Saka in central Asia.

530 BCE

Scythian Massagetes kill Cyrus the Great.

c. 520 BCE

Darius defeats "Saka tigrakhauda" (Scythians with pointed hats).

c. 512 BCE

Darius invades Scythia northwest of the Black Sea.

c. 400–325 BCE

High point of Scythian power.

325 BCE

Scythians defeat a Macedonian army sent by Alexander

c. 300 BCE

Scythians ousted from northern Balkans by the Celts.

c. 130 BCE

Scythians are absorbed into Sarmatian tribes.

SCYTHIAN HORSEMANSHIP

The Scythians were among the first peoples to ride horses in battle. Scythians rode without stirrups, their legs gripped the animal low on its belly. They trained their horses to kneel so that men could remount quickly. Scythian archers cut their horses' manes short so the manes would not get tangled in their bowstrings. They left only a few long tufts around the shoulder bones, which the riders used as grips to direct the horse.

The Scythian habit of eating and sleeping on horseback may have led to the Greek legend of the half-horse, half-human Centaur. The Scythians favored chestnut-colored horses, which they believed had harder hooves than horses with white markings. Horse designs often appear on Scythian drinking vessels and bowls. Horse meat was eaten at funeral feasts, and archaeologists have found horse skeletons in many Scythian graves. One grave, found at Aul Ul in the Caucasus, held the skeletons of 360 slaughtered horses laid out carefully in rows and circles.

▶ *This fourth-century-BCE golden plaque shows a Scythian horseman brandishing a spear.*

The fast-raiding Scythians were a constant threat to the more settled peoples around them. They invaded Mesopotamia and Syria in the seventh century BCE, reaching as far south as the kingdom of Judah. The great Persian king Cyrus the Great died in 530 BCE fighting the Scythian tribe of Massagetes on his northern frontier. Darius launched a major invasion of Scythia in 512 BCE, but the tribes retreated at the sight of his vast army. Alexander the Great also tried to conquer the Scythians, but their horse archers destroyed the experienced Macedonian army in 325 BCE.

The Scythians were finally overcome by the Celts and Sarmatians, peoples who shared their nomadic lifestyle. Around 130 BCE the Scythians were mostly absorbed into new groups of tribes and vanished from history.

Scythian Customs

Scythian men often took more than one wife. Unlike Sarmatian women, who fought alongside their menfolk, Scythian women busied themselves with domestic tasks and child rearing. They traveled with their families in wagons as the tribe followed its herds. The most important constituent of the Scythians' diet was koumiss (fermented mare's milk). They used trained dogs to hunt game and caught quantities of a large spineless fish called *antakaeos*, which they pickled with salt collected at the mouths of the rivers along the Black Sea coast.

▶ *Despite their nomadic lifestyle, the Scythians were skilled craftsmen. This perfectly spherical cup from the sixth century BCE shows scenes from daily life in Scythia. Here an injured Scythian receives treatment from a comrade who bandages his leg.*

The Greeks and Persians were horrified by some of the more brutal Scythian customs. Scythian warriors scalped the enemies that they killed in battle. The scalps were cleaned and worn on their belts as a sign of bravery. Sometimes the scalps were sewn together to form a cloak. Human skin was also used to make quivers for their arrows and a covering for their possessions in their wagons. Prisoners were sacrificed to the Scythian god of war. Their skulls were cleaned and lined with leather so they could be used as goblets. Rich Scythians sometimes lined these skulls with gold and used them in banquets or when offering wine to honored guests.

Scythian kings were mummified when they died. The belly of the royal corpse was slit open, cleaned out, and filled with sweet-smelling herbs and preserving waxes. The body was then taken by wagon around the tribal homelands so that all could pay their respects to the dead king. Finally the body was lowered into a great pit. The king's favorite servants were strangled and laid by his side. The grave was then covered in a tumulus, a high earthen burial mound.

In recent years Russian and Ukrainian archaeologists have found rich treasures in royal Scythian graves, known as kurgans, along the coast of the Black Sea.

SEE ALSO

- Alexander the Great • Celts
- Cyrus the Great • Darius I
- Herodotus

The Greek historian Herodotus reported that Scythian warriors drank a mixture of wine and blood in ceremonies when they swore oaths to each other.

Sennacherib

Sennacherib (the English form of the name Sîn-ahhe-eriba, which means "Sîn has replaced his brothers") was king of Assyria from 704 to 681 BCE. He was the son of the warlike Sargon II and as a young man commanded the armies along Assyria's frontiers with the kingdoms of Urartu and Media. As a ruler Sennacherib was a cultured patron of architecture, science, and agriculture. His reign was a period of prosperity that has been called the *pax Assyrica* (Assyrian peace).

Despite the fact that Sennacherib appeared less interested in warfare than most other kings of Assyria, he was still a good soldier and a successful general, and much of his reign was spent crushing rebellions against his rule by peoples on the edges of his kingdom.

The War in Judah

In 701 BCE Sennacherib set out to put down a rebellion in Syria, Palestine, and Judah, where Assyrian vassal territories had taken up arms after the death of Sargon II. Much is known about Sennacherib's war against Judah because it was recorded in the Old Testament as well as on a well-preserved series of bas-reliefs in his palace at Nineveh. The reliefs show the Assyrian army besieging and capturing the fortress of Lachish. Sennacherib also besieged Jerusalem until a plague fell on his troops and forced him to retreat. Sennacherib captured thousands of Hebrews and took them back to Assyria as slaves.

▶ *Sennacherib personally supervised the siege of the Hebrew fortress of Lachish in 701 BCE. Bas-relief sculptures at Nineveh tell the story of the siege. This panel shows Sennacherib giving orders to his officers.*

In November 689 BCE Sennacherib recaptured the city of Babylon, which had rebelled against his rule. Angry after an expensive fifteen-month siege, he ordered the destruction of the city. Although it was an ancient and sacred place, he leveled the buildings and flooded the site, possibly by diverting the Euphrates River. Sennacherib later boasted about this dreadful act:

Like a hurricane I attacked the city and like a storm I overthrew it. . . . I spared none of its people, young or old, and I filled the streets of the city with their corpses. I devastated the town and its houses from the foundations to the roofs . . . So that even the soil of its temples be forgotten in the future, I ravaged the land with water and turned it into pastures. . . . I removed the dust of Babylon. . . . and stored some of it in a covered jar in the Temple of the New Year Festival in Assur.

Cited in D. D. Luckenbill, *Ancient Records of Assyria and Babylonia*, Vol. 11

Pax Assyrica

Assyrian kings had traditionally set out to wage war every spring, when the marching season arrived. However, records of only eight campaigns in Sennacherib's twenty-four-year reign survive.

Sennacherib spent much time restoring the ancient city of Nineveh, which he chose to be his capital. He built dams, canals, and aqueducts to carry water to the city and to irrigate the surrounding fields. The fertile grain farms around Nineveh were needed to feed the city's rapidly growing population. Sennacherib also ordered the building of temples and other public works around his kingdom.

Assassination

In January 681 BCE, while praying in a temple at Nineveh, Sennacherib was murdered by two of his own sons, who had been passed over in the search for a successor. One writer says he was stabbed, while another says that he was crushed to death under a gigantic statue of a winged bull.

The Hebrews believed that he had been punished by Yahweh, the God of Israel, while the Babylonians said that their god Marduk had avenged their devastated city. After his death Assyria was plunged into constant wars that lasted until its final destruction in 612 BCE.

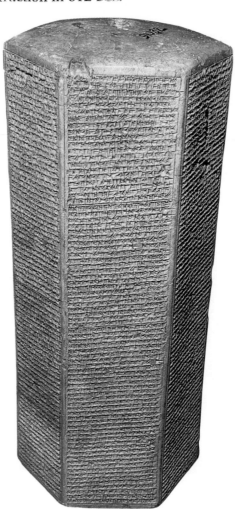

◄ This hexagonal clay tablet, discovered in the ruins of Nineveh in 1830, tells of Sennacherib's campaigns against the Hittites and the kingdoms of Judah and Israel in the early eighth century BCE.

SEE ALSO
- Assyrians
- Babylon
- Marduk • Nineveh

Ships and Boats

Historians and archaeologists believe the earliest people to cross large stretches of water, perhaps as long ago as the Neolithic era (c. 8000–4000 BCE), used logs. At the next stage, these logs were hollowed out to make canoes. By 3500 BCE the Egyptians were using oars and sometimes sails to propel their boats along the Nile.

Egyptian boats were made of papyrus and reeds woven together with string. A large oar at the stern steered the boat. The bigger vessels also had square sails, held aloft by a central mast. By 2700 BCE Egyptian ships were strong enough to carry stone to build monuments.

At the same time, the people of Mesopotamia were using *gufas*—basket-like boats made of woven reeds and pitched with tar to make them waterproof—to navigate the Tigris and Euphrates Rivers.

Wooden Ships

The oldest surviving ship yet uncovered was found near the Great Pyramid at Giza. Made of cedar and sycamore, it was built around 2600 BCE. As Egypt grew richer and traders were able to buy wood in larger quantities, Egyptian boat builders developed long, flat-bottomed barges.

Phoenician Ships

The ancient world's most powerful ships were built by the Phoenicians, traders who were famed for their navigational skills. Phoenicia occupied a narrow strip of land on the eastern coast of the Mediterranean, and all its major cities were ports.

The Phoenicians were the first to build ships with keels and ribs. The masts on their craft were made from cedar and the sails from Egyptian linen, which could withstand strong winds and storms.

The Phoenician cargo ships' round hulls helped them move through the water faster than any other boat. Their use of sails freed space formerly used by oarsmen, so more goods could fit on board. The Phoenicians also developed biremes and triremes, galleys with two and three rows of oars, respectively, on either side.

▼ *This funerary boat was used to ferry the Egyptian pharaoh Khufu (c. 2600 BCE) to his final resting place in the Great Pyramid at Giza. During his lifetime, the king might also have used the boat to travel up and down the Nile River during festivals.*

Greek Ships

At the same time that the Phoenicians were setting up trading posts, the people of Crete were also beginning to establish themselves in the eastern Mediterranean. They built strong, narrow warships with which they defended their cities, which were close to the water.

By the fifth century BCE, the Greeks had conquered many surrounding countries by annihilating enemy navies. They spent years perfecting their warships, which were made of curved wooden boards pinned to a solid framework. The stern was raised to protect the captain and the officers. Ropes along the ship helped keep the galley in one piece as it rammed the enemy.

Greek crews usually numbered 220, of whom 170 were skilled oarsmen. Their aim was to plow into the enemy's oars as soldiers boarded the enemy vessel. Most Greek war-

ships had a secret weapon— an underwater battering ram hidden from view.

Roman Ships

Between 264 and 241 BCE the Romans adapted the Greek warship for use in the Punic Wars—battles between the Romans and the Carthaginians for supremacy in the Mediterranean. Roman galleys were made stronger with leather and cloth soaked in vinegar, which shielded against fires.

▲ *This wall painting, found in Thera on the Greek island of Santorini and dating from the thirteenth century BCE, shows Minoan ships being rowed into port, surrounded by dolphins, animals considered to be sailors' friends.*

IN THIS ACCOUNT FROM THE OLD TESTAMENT, HIRAM, THE KING OF THE PHOENICIAN PORT OF TYRE, WRITES TO KING SOLOMON ABOUT TRANSPORTING TIMBERS FOR BUILDING THE FAMOUS JEWISH TEMPLE:

My servants shall bring them down to Lebanon unto the sea, and I will convey them by the sea in floats unto the place that thou shall appoint me.

1 KINGS 5:9 (KJV)

Roman ships had a *corvus*, a plank that was used as a walkway when moving from one ship to another or boarding captured vessels. The *corvus* was also used to make captured soldiers walk into the water. Their heavy armor would pull them to the bottom of the sea, and they would drown. The *corvus* was the inspiration behind the notorious pirates' plank. Roman galleys also had giant catapults, used to hurl burning ammunition.

The Romans used different ships for traveling and trade. These vessels had curved hulls and no oars and relied on sails for movement. Roman ships traveled constantly across the Mediterranean Sea to transport goods. By the time of the decline of the Roman Empire, the Mediterranean seabed was littered with such ships sunk in storms. They and their remaining cargo afford modern scholars a unique chance to study the practices of ancient mariners.

LAPITA NAVIGATION

The Lapita people set off from Southeast Asia to colonize the Pacific islands around 1500 BCE. They traveled in double canoes lashed together with plant fiber and equipped with outriggers—wooden platforms on which were carried plants, food, and animals. Highly accomplished navigators, the Lapita were guided by the sun, the stars, and currents and swells; they propelled their boats by using paddles and small sails.

In 1500 BCE the Lapita people reached the Bismarck Archipelago. By 1300 BCE they reached Tonga, and around 1000 BCE they landed on Samoa. From there the descendants of the Lapita pushed on until they reached Easter Island around 400 CE. It is difficult for modern historians to understand quite how the Lapita people crossed so many hundreds of miles of ocean in little more than hollowed-out tree trunks.

▶ This marble relief, part of an ancient Roman sarcophagus carved in either the second or third century CE, shows Roman ships battling through rough seas.

SEE ALSO
- Migration
- Phoenicians
- Transportation
- Tyre

Shulgi

Shulgi was king of the Mesopotamian city of Ur for forty-seven years, probably from 2094 to 2047 BCE. His father, Ur-Nammu, had established control over southern Mesopotamia and founded a new dynasty of five rulers, including himself. The dynasty governed until 2004 BCE.

Shulgi took the throne at a young age, after his father was killed in battle. The fact that little is known about the early years of Shulgi's reign itself probably indicates a period of peaceful rule. During Shulgi's reign the land of the Elamites was conquered, but generally speaking, the Mesopotamian king established diplomatic relations with neighboring lands, and trade was conducted peacefully.

Royal Hymns

Archaeologists have uncovered a number of royal hymns to Shulgi that are thought to have formed part of ceremonial occasions at the court of the king. Shulgi is praised for his strength and intelligence, and his hunting skills are demonstrated by his ability to fight lions single-handed.

Shulgi is also praised for his artistic talents, for his refined singing voice, and for his ability to master a number of musical instruments. One hymn gives a voice to Shulgi himself, and he boasts of his mathematical skills: "No one can write a tablet like me . . . adding, subtracting, counting, and accounting."

The Lunar Eclipse

Shulgi's reign ended violently with his murder by his son, Amar-Sin. The event was associated with an eclipse of the moon, a phenomenon that occurs when the earth passes between the sun and the moon and prevents the moon from reflecting the sun's light. The earliest known references to eclipses are found on astrological tablets from Ur, and they warn that eclipses are signs of disaster to come.

▼ This Babylonian terracotta jar, dating from around 1700 BCE, shows Ishtar, the goddess of love and war, whose association with Shulgi emphasized his power.

This black basalt plaque dates from the twenty-first century BCE. Its inscription, in the wedge-shaped marks of Sumerian cuneiform, commemorates Shulgi's achievements.

SEE ALSO

• Elamites • Ishtar
• Mesopotamia
• Ur

One astrological tablet warns of the events to come: "The king of Ur will see a famine, there will be many deaths, the king of Ur will be wronged by his son; the son who has wronged his father, the Sun-god will catch him, and he will die at the burial of his father." The eclipse referred to on the tablet has been dated as probably occurring on April 4, 2094 BCE, the year Shulgi assumed the throne.

THE FOLLOWING IS FROM A ROYAL HYMN GLORIFYING SHULGI. IT WAS WRITTEN IN THE SUMERIAN LANGUAGE AND WAS MOST PROBABLY SUNG TO ACCOMPANY A DANCE AT A ROYAL OCCASION.

May the king's name be pre-eminent for future times, may the message of Shulgi, king of Ur, the song of his strength, the song of his might, the eternal message of his all-surpassing wisdom, be transmitted to posterity for future times.

CITED IN GWENDOLYN LEICK, MESOPOTAMIA

After Shulgi's death the kingdom began to weaken, and his grandson Ibbi-Sin was carried off a prisoner to Elam in about 2004 BCE.

Divine Status

Shulgi's power as the ruler of Ur was reinforced by his association with the gods. As king, Shulgi had a divine status. In Mesopotamian literature, he is portrayed as the husband or lover of the powerful goddess Ishtar. One written account describes how Shulgi visited all the shrines in his kingdom.

Such visits could have been occasion for public displays, celebrating the king's authority and proclaiming the blessing he receives from the gods. Shulgi's relations with the priests of the temples may not always have been harmonious because halfway through his reign he took control of most of the temples in his kingdom and collected taxes from them.

Skara Brae, Orkney

The prehistoric village of Skara Brae is the oldest and best-preserved neolithic settlement in northern Europe. The five-thousand-year-old cluster of stone houses is situated on Orkney, the biggest of a group of islands off the northeastern coast of Scotland.

Discovery of the Site

In 1850 a storm stripped the grass off a sand dune known locally as Skara Brae. Buried inside were the ruins of ancient buildings unlike any known from elsewhere on the islands. As the sand was removed, a village was revealed. Further excavations were carried out in the 1920s, and a sea wall was built to prevent the site from being washed away.

The Buildings of Skara Brae

It appears that people lived at Skara Brae for about six hundred years, from around 3100 until around 2500 BCE, during which time its buildings were periodically demolished and new ones built. The village consisted of small rectangular houses, of which nine survive.

Built from stone, the houses stood close together; narrow passages wound between them. House walls were around three feet (1 m) thick, and a low doorway was the only way in and out. Roofs were probably made from turf laid on timber or whale-bone frames. In the center of each house was an open fire that burned on the floor. Around the walls were pieces of furniture formed from flat slabs of stone—cupboards, seats, and box beds.

Everyday Life in Skara Brae

How many people lived at Skara Brae at any one time? The small number of houses suggests it may have been only a few families that subsisted on farming—growing wheat and barley in small fields and raising cattle, sheep, and pigs.

◀ Inside a house at Skara Brae. In the center of the floor is a hearth, and against the walls are a cupboard and a box bed, all made from local stone.

ORKNEY'S PREHISTORIC LANDSCAPE

The Orkney Islands contain Europe's greatest concentration of prehistoric sites for the period 3000 BCE to 400 CE, including standing stones and stone circles. The widest stone circle is the Ring of Brodgar, whose stones (twenty-seven of the original sixty still stand) mark out a circle 341 feet (104 m) across. Nearby, the Stones of Stenness form a smaller circle, but the towering stones stand some nineteen feet (5.8 m) high.

Throughout the islands are the remains of several chambered cairns, prehistoric tombs in which the burial chamber is covered by a cairn, or mound, of stones. The most famous burial mound is Maes Howe, whose grass-covered hump, twenty-five feet (7.5 m) high, contains a burial chamber built of stone at the end of a passage. Between 200 and 400 CE, toward the close of the prehistoric period in Orkney, brochs—round towers made from stone but without mortar—were built. Experts believe people may have used them to shelter from danger.

▲ A standing stone in the Ring of Brodgar. Other stones from this great circle can be seen in the distance.

The people of Skara Brae used grain from their crops to bake bread and brew beer. They sailed offshore to catch deep-water cod, which they fished using limpets as bait. Crabs, oysters, and seabirds were also eaten, as were red deer and puffballs (a type of fungus).

Tools were made from stone and bone; beads and pendants were crafted from bone and shell. At night house doors were closed, and the occupants slept on heather, furs, and skins packed into their stone-lined beds.

The End of the Village

When Skara Brae was excavated, archaeologists found signs it had been abandoned in a hurry, though it did not appear to have been attacked by raiders. The evidence led them to believe a disaster, such as a great storm, had overwhelmed the village, destroying some houses and burying those that remained under sand.

SEE ALSO

• Hunting and Fishing • Prehistory

Slavery

Slavery—the ownership of people—was a fact of life in the majority of ancient societies. Slaves were their owner's property and could be bought, sold, or given away. Slaves had very few rights; they could not, for example, inherit property. On the other hand, many early civilizations had detailed codes of how slaves were to be treated, and few civilizations allowed slave owners to kill a slave for no reason.

Slavery and Civilization

In general, the practice of slavery was restricted to more advanced rather than primitive civilizations in the ancient world. Two conditions were necessary for slavery to function. The first was a hierarchy, that is, a society arranged into different levels, or classes, with powerful rulers and priests at the top and powerless prisoners and slaves at the bottom. The second was spare wealth. A family could maintain a kitchen slave, for example, only if it could afford to feed and clothe him or her.

The practice of slavery was virtually impossible in very primitive societies, because they were not highly organized and had little or no surplus wealth.

Ancient Views of Slavery

There is very little historical evidence of what most people thought of slavery, largely because slavery was accepted as a normal part of everyday life. From the earliest times, however, there were concerns that it was morally wrong to treat people as property. Slaves who were treated cruelly hated their situation and were often prepared to run away or rebel.

Some ancient societies expressed their doubts about slavery in their literature. Many Greek writers held the view that the ideal condition for a human being is freedom. Yet, though it was not permitted for an Athenian citizen to be enslaved, most Athenians owned non-Athenian slaves.

◀ This scene, carved on a pillar at a theater in Libya (North Africa) in 180 CE, shows two actors performing a scene in which a slave is scolded by his master.

▲ An ancient Greek terra-cotta model of a slave girl cooking.

instances of people selling themselves into slavery for the same reasons.

People could either be made slaves or born slaves. Enslavement was often a punishment for criminals and debtors. The child of two slaves or, more commonly, the child of a slave woman and her master, was a born slave (Aesop, the famous Greek fable writer, was probably born a slave). Still, there were examples in ancient Greece and Rome of children born to slave women being granted their freedom and inheriting their father's property and leading lives of fame and fortune.

India and China

Slavery existed in ancient India, where it was first recorded in the first century BCE. Records of slavery in China go back much farther, to the Shang dynasty of the eighteenth to twelfth centuries BCE.

In China, however, slavery did not affect more than about 5 percent of the population. Peasants, not slaves, did the ordinary manual labor. Slaves were expensive luxuries of the ruling classes.

Slaves in Egypt

Slavery seems not to have been widespread in Egypt before the period of Greek rule known as the Ptolemaic period (332–30 BCE). Slaves were usually prisoners of war. Some were treated well, and it was even possible for male slaves to marry freeborn women and to own land.

Under the pharaohs most of the population was tied to the land, and given that fact, people were often included as part of the possessions of an estate. Nevertheless, these people were not strictly slaves, as they were tied to the land by tradition rather than by law.

Acquiring Slaves

Slaves were acquired in a variety of ways. The most common was through war. Slaves might be captured during fighting (as happened frequently in Africa), or they might be given to the victor by his defeated enemy. The Roman general Julius Caesar became a very wealthy man from the large numbers of slaves he acquired from his campaigns in Gaul (modern-day France) in the first century BCE.

Pirates and kidnappers sold their victims into slavery to get money. There were also many examples in early civilizations of people selling relatives, especially children, into slavery to raise money for food or to pay debts. There were even

Greece and Rome

All western Asian civilizations kept slaves. They feature in the Bible and in the Babylonian law code of Hammurabi that dates from about 1750 BCE. Perhaps the best-known slave-based societies were ancient Greece and Rome. The whole of Athenian culture until the sixth century BCE was based on slavery. In fact, there were as many slaves as there were free citizens. Slaves were vital to the city's economy. This system allowed the wealthy classes the leisure to create the glories of Greek culture.

NEARLY ALL RELIGIONS URGE MASTERS TO TREAT SLAVES KINDLY. THE OLD TESTAMENT CONTAINS DETAILED RULES ABOUT THE FAIR TREATMENT OF SLAVES. SAINT PAUL, ONE OF THE MOST IMPORTANT EARLY CHRISTIANS, MADE IT CLEAR IN HIS LETTERS THAT, BETWEEN CHRISTIANS, ALL SOCIAL DISTINCTIONS ARE FALSE:

For through faith you are all sons of God in union with Christ Jesus. Baptised into union with him, you have all put on Christ as a garment. There is no such thing as Jew and Greek, slave and freeman, male and female; for you are all one person in Jesus Christ.

GALATIANS 3:26–28 (NEW ENGLISH BIBLE)

▼ *This gold-covered stuccoed-wood image—enslaved prisoners from one of Egypt's wars—was carved on a chariot found in Tutankhamen's tomb.*

Spartacus

Roman slavery is well documented in the exploits of the best-known slave rebel: Spartacus, the gladiator who defied the might of Rome in the first century BCE. Leading a huge warrior band of runaway slaves, he defeated several Roman armies and devastated much of Italy. Spartacus and his fellow rebels were finally captured and crucified in 71 BCE.

People in later civilizations campaigning for the abolition of slavery have used Spartacus as a heroic figurehead.

The Treatment of Slaves

The conditions of slavery varied from one early civilization to another. The slaves that endured the worst treatment were probably those who worked in the mines of Greece, Rome, and Egypt. Laboring in frightful conditions and often maltreated, few mine workers lived to see middle age.

In other societies slaves were treated better, and household slaves often became part of the family with whom they lived and worked. In India, China, and other civilizations, slaves often earned respect for their musical or artistic talents. Furthermore, most societies allowed slaves to acquire their freedom, either by purchase or as a gift from their owner.

◀ This seventh-century-BCE stone relief from the palace of Sennacherib at Nineveh (in present-day Iraq) shows prisoners working as slaves in a stone quarry, probably for the construction of the palace itself.

SEE ALSO
- Social Hierarchy
- Spartacus

Social Hierarchy

A social hierarchy is the organization of people in a society into different levels, known as ranks, orders, or classes. Enforcement of a social hierarchy is one method by which rulers maintain law and order, and so social rank was often emphasized after periods of disorder. Rulers expected hierarchy to keep their kingdom peaceful and stable.

Many ancient societies were organized in similar ways and commonly had four main levels. These levels were based on what people did for their community. At the top were the leaders, who ran the society. Beneath them was an educated class of learned men such as government officials and priests. The majority of freemen belonged to the third level of craftsmen, traders, merchants, and farmers. The bottom group was made up of slaves, prisoners of war, and criminals.

Signs of Rank

Ancient societies showed social rank in a number of ways. Nobles from the Mayan cultures in ancient Mexico and the Moche culture of ancient Peru wore decorative metal plates through their noses. Senators in republican Rome wore a toga with a broad purple stripe, while ordinary Romans were allowed to wear only a plain white toga. Distinguished Roman military leaders wore a toga with two thin stripes.

Common men in ancient Greece wore a short tunic called a chiton. It was easy to wear and maintain and did not get in the way when a person was doing everyday jobs. However, men and women from highborn Greek families wore a long robe called a pallium, which was heavy to wear and had many complicated folds. Wearing a pallium was a sign to others that one had the time and the slaves to keep it looking clean and elegant.

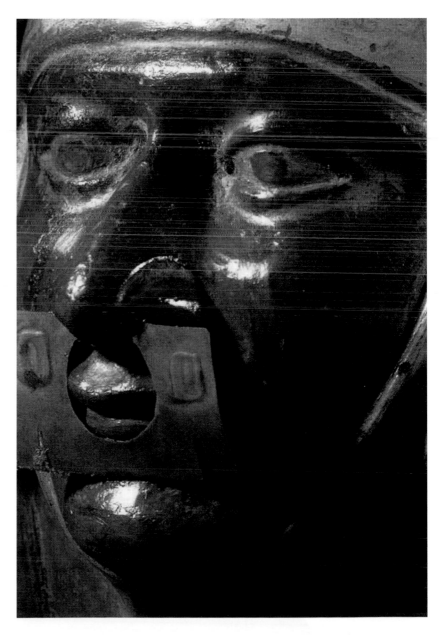

▼ High-ranking members of society in the Moche culture (who lived in present-day Peru between 200 and 800 CE) displayed their rank with jewelry worn around the nose.

It is wrong for a gentleman of high rank to know about ordinary everyday things, but right and proper for him to carry responsibility for matters of great importance. It is wrong for an ordinary man to be entrusted with great responsibility, but right and proper for him to know about menial matters.

CONFUCIUS, ANALECTS

▼ *Among the barbarian tribes, wergild was calculated in solidi, or silver shillings. This solidus was minted by Theodoric the Great (c. 454– 526 CE), an Ostrogothic king of Italy.*

Social rank among the Goths depended on the fame that a man and his kinsmen won in battle. The Goths considered wisdom a more valuable quality in a leader than power or wealth. A Gothic king was obeyed only if he ruled wisely; he would then be blessed by the gods with victories and good harvests.

Responsibilities of High Rank

People of high rank were usually expected to do more for their community in return for their privileges. In ancient China the great landowners had absolute power over the subjects who lived on their land. However, these nobles had to serve the emperor with complete obedience and provide him with a certain number of armed men each year.

Only citizens of Athens were allowed to vote in the city assembly or to speak in the law courts, but first they had to do two years service in the army when they reached the age of eighteen. In Babylon members of the *amelu,* or patrician, class enjoyed many privileges, but they had to pay higher fines if they broke the law. Babylonian nobles were executed by impalement (whereby a stake is driven through the body) if they committed the most serious crimes. Punishments were heavier for Babylonian nobles because more was expected of them.

SEE ALSO

• Aryans • China • Clothes • Hinduism
• Roman Republic and Empire

Socrates

The teacher and philosopher Socrates (c. 470–399 BCE) is one of the most important figures of ancient Greece. Together with Plato and Aristotle, Socrates is credited with laying the philosophical foundations of Western culture. His life and ideas have had a profound effect on the work of many important thinkers in history.

Historical Knowledge of Socrates

Socrates himself wrote nothing. What is known about him comes from the writings of others, especially from Plato, his most famous pupil. Plato considered him a hero. However, Aristophanes mocked Socrates in his plays, and Eupolis, another dramatist, portrayed him as untrustworthy.

Socrates' father was a stonemason. Socrates married, had a son, and served in the Athenian army. Writers describe him as charming and easygoing but capable of great physical endurance. Sculptures show him as ugly and pug-nosed.

Socrates' Teaching

The philosophical ideas of Socrates have been preserved in Plato's dialogues and in his dramatizations of Socrates in action. Therefore, it can be difficult to distinguish between Plato's views and Socrates' views. When Socrates argues with someone about courage, the best kind of education, or true justice, Plato's voice can also be heard.

Unlike earlier Greek philosophers, who asked questions about the physical world and science, Socrates was concerned with what is right and wrong about human behavior. For Socrates right and wrong are dependent on ignorance and wisdom. The basis of living well is knowledge and wisdom. The phrase *know thyself*, which was inscribed at the entrance to the famous temple at Delphi, was a guiding principle in Socrates' life.

Socrates also taught that it was very difficult to know anything for certain. He insisted that he knew nothing, and his questioning of others often showed that they knew much less than they thought they did.

▼ *This marble bust of Socrates is probably the work of Lysippus, the famous sculptor and painter patronized by Alexander the Great.*

▲ In this dramatic eighteenth-century painting, Socrates, still speaking and gesturing, accepts the bowl of poisonous hemlock, while some friends turn away, unable to watch.

Socrates' Death

Socrates' followers included some who helped put the Thirty Tyrants in control in Athens in 404 BCE. When the Athenians restored democracy in 399, the leaders of the 404 revolution were outlawed. Socrates became a target of the democrats. He was accused of corrupting the young and of introducing new gods without the approval of the religious authorities.

At his trial Socrates defended himself, but he was found guilty. He was invited to suggest a punishment, a common procedure in such cases. Socrates suggested that he should be given a pension for life. Instead he was sentenced to death and forced to drink hemlock, a deadly poison.

Protest

Many Athenians protested and wrote in defense of Socrates. Plato's tragic story, based on the actual events of the time, is told in three episodes: the trial, a visit to Socrates in prison, and finally Socrates' moving death. Plato shows Socrates refusing to admit guilt or ask for a lesser sentence and dying for his right to speak the truth.

SOCRATES DEFENDS HIMSELF IN FRONT OF THE ATHENIAN JURY:

That is the kind of thing they say. And that is the kind of thing you yourselves have seen in the comedy of Aristophanes, where a certain man named Socrates comes on stage, whirling around, claiming he can walk on the air, waffling on like a simpleton saying he knows many other crazy things—about which I have to confess I know absolutely nothing. . . . I challenge any of you, that if you ever heard me say anything about such matters as I'm accused of, to speak out now.

PLATO, APOLOGY

SEE ALSO

- Athens • Greece, Classical
- Greek Philosophy • Plato

Solon

In the sixth century BCE the Greeks who lived in Athens turned to one wise man to help lead them out of a crisis in their government. That wise man was Solon, who, as chief lawgiver, introduced many reforms to the Athenian system of government. As ancient Greek historical records begin long after the death of Solon, more is known about his deeds than his life.

Crisis

Solon was born in Athens and may have worked as a merchant for a time. When Solon reached adulthood, Athens was ruled by an aristocracy, a small select band of nobles who selected nine magistrates, called archons, to govern and judge for a year. Harsh laws created around 620 BCE by a previous ruler, Draco, were in force. Even small crimes, such as the theft of food, were punishable by death. Problems in the Athenian economy were causing widespread poverty, especially among farmers and peasants. Some sold themselves into slavery to repay debts. The ordinary people of Athens struggled to survive and had few freedoms. Resentment grew and with it the threat of violence and chaos.

Elected To Reform

According to many sources, Solon was chosen as a chief lawgiver in 594 BCE and was given wide-ranging powers to reform the way in which Athens was run. Solon championed the cause of the *hektomoroi*, landowners who paid one-sixth of their produce to the aristocrats but were excluded from government.

Solon immediately made more dramatic changes than had been expected. He canceled all outstanding debts and freed many Athenians from slavery. He also banned moneylenders from threatening borrowers with slavery if they did not repay their loan. Solon reformed many other laws and removed the death sentence except for the most serious crimes.

◄ In this late-seventeenth-century painting Solon is depicted arguing that his proposed reforms are just.

▶ Introduced after the death of Solon, this ancient Greek device, called a kleroterion, was used to select jurors to sit on courts in Athens.

SEE ALSO
• Athens
• Greece, Classical

Some Power to the People: Structural Changes

Solon divided Athenian society into four classes based on wealth and property. Only the two richest classes could become archons. The Areopagus (council of nobles), whose members were ex-archons, supervised the archons. The third class could serve on an elected council of four hundred, while the fourth and poorest class could elect certain officials. They could also take part in an assembly called the *ecclesia*, which voted on matters brought to it by the council of four hundred. These reforms are considered to be the first attempt at a type of government now known as democracy.

Solon's Legacy

Solon upset many people with his reforms, which were thought to go too far by some—generally rich and aristocratic Athenians—and not far enough by others. However, the reforms remained in place for a number of years and went some way to creating a fairer way of life in Athens. Over time, however, quarrels between the different classes returned. In 546 BCE, after failing in two previous attempts, Peisistratos finally swept to power and ruled as tyrant, or sole leader, until his death in 528 BCE. He restored order partly through tougher laws, yet he kept many of Solon's reforms in place.

SOLON EXPLAINS HIS VIEWS AND DEEDS:

And others had been shamefully made slaves
Right here, trembling at the tempers of their masters.
These I set free. I put these things in force
By joining might and right together
And I carried through as I had promised.
I wrote laws, too, equally for poor and rich,
And made justice that is fit and straight for all.

SOLON

Sparta

The ancestors of the Spartans were among the Dorian tribes who settled in the Peloponnese area of southern Greece, in particular Laconia, around 1000 BCE. The culture of the native population had included an early writing system, which fell out of use as the settlers came to dominate. Spartans are famed for their courage and aggressiveness, which may have sprung from the need to keep neighboring tribes under control.

In 720 BCE the Spartans conquered the Messenians, who lived to the west of Laconia. The Spartans annexed the Messenian territory and treated the Messenians almost like slaves.

By 700 BCE Sparta was developing much as other Greek city-states did. The Spartans made elegant pottery and became known for their poets and musicians. They traded with other Greeks and produced fine athletes at the Olympic Games.

Around this time the Messenians—known as Helots in some Greek sources—rebelled. In order to maintain its dominance, Sparta began to develop into a military power. After a series of campaigns in the second half of the sixth century BCE, the Spartans had secured a dominant position in the Peloponnese and beyond.

The Spartan Regime

From the middle of the sixth century, inequality between the Spartans and the Laconians and Helots increased. Despite this disparity, Spartan citizens were known as Equals.

The Spartan authorities began to turn all Spartan men into soldiers. At the age of seven, boys went to military boarding school, where reading and writing were of little importance. Boys were encouraged to form gangs and brawl in the streets.

Neighboring Greeks claimed the Spartans had beating competitions, where the winner was the last to cry out, and that some boys died rather than submit. However, as the Spartans left no records, such stories cannot be proved.

▼ A sculpture of Leonidas, King of Sparta, who died with three hundred Spartans defending the narrow pass of Thermopylae against the Persians in 480 BCE.

SPARTAN WORDS

Two words in the English language come from *Sparta*. Laconic *describes a way of speaking using few words, a habit associated with Spartans.* Spartan *refers to a simple way of life, without luxuries or comforts.*

At twenty-four, training was complete, and the Spartan male became an Equal. At thirty he could leave the army, marry, and vote in the Assembly of Equals.

Men and Women

As an infant a male Spartan was granted a piece of land by the state that was his until he died. Helots worked the land for him. More skilled tasks such as armor making and blacksmithing were the responsibilities of the more respected *perioikoi*.

Women were encouraged to be fit so that they would produce healthy children. Girls trained in physical fitness, sometimes alongside the boys. Spinning and weaving were regarded as beneath them.

Government

Sparta had two kings, who were religious and military leaders. Only one went to war at a time. They were advised by a council of elders and five elected officials called ephors. The ephors made sure the state functioned smoothly and had the power to depose kings. The Assembly of Equals voted on important decisions not by a show of hands but by shouting.

Sparta and Greece

When the Persians invaded Greece, the Spartans arrived too late for the Battle of Marathon (490 BCE). The Spartans then put up a brave but doomed defense at Thermopylae (480 BCE).

Fifty years later Sparta won a long conflict with Athens, known as the Peloponnesian War (431–404 BCE). Shortly afterward Spartan power declined, until the final defeat of the Spartans by the Thebans at the Battle of Leuctra (371 BCE).

▶ *This map shows the conflicting city-states of the Greek-speaking world in the Peloponnesian War (431–404 BCE).*

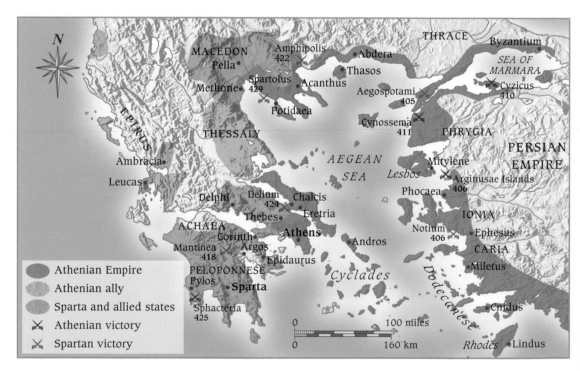

SEE ALSO

- Athens
- Greece, Classical

Spartacus

Spartacus has become an almost legendary figure: the slave who defied the might of Rome from 73 to 71 BCE. After leaving the Roman army, Spartacus was captured and sold into slavery. He was trained as a gladiator and then escaped. Spartacus soon amassed a huge army of slaves who defeated the Roman army several times and almost completed an astonishing march to freedom.

According to modern and classical historians, Spartacus came from Thrace, a region of northern Greece. He may have served in the Roman army fighting in Macedonia (part of modern-day Greece, Yugoslavia, and Bulgaria). Spartacus left the army without permission and was captured and sold into slavery. A gladiator trainer named Lentulus Batiatus bought Spartacus and trained him at his gladiator school near Capua in Italy.

The Fight for Freedom

In 73 BCE Spartacus escaped with around seventy other gladiators. They managed to steal some weapons and camped on the slopes of Mount Vesuvius, near Naples. There they were joined by large numbers of other slaves from the surrounding region. Spartacus believed that his slave army could fight its way to freedom by marching north and leaving Italy altogether.

To the amazement and shame of the Roman senate and its military commanders, Spartacus's forces defeated two Roman armies in 73 BCE and another three in 72. They laid waste to southern Italy and, as they went along, liberated more and more slaves, who joined the march north. Some sources estimate that Spartacus's army numbered 120,000 men, along with many of their women and children.

◀ The American actor Kirk Douglas as Spartacus in Stanley Kubrick's classic 1960 film.

MARCUS CRASSUS *C. 112–53 BCE*

Marcus Licinius Crassus was an extremely wealthy Roman nobleman and general. In 59 BCE, twelve years after his defeat of Spartacus, Crassus formed an alliance with the generals Julius Caesar and Gnaeus Pompeius Magnus (Pompey). He was useful to them because of his wealth, but he wanted to prove himself their equal as a great general. He set off to campaign in the east and invaded Mesopotamia (modern-day Iraq). The expedition ended in disaster when he was killed and his army was defeated.

▶ Thracian gladiators, such as Spartacus, are believed to have worn helmets like this one, made from solid bronze and dating from the first century CE.

In 72 BCE Spartacus's army reached the northern border of Italy. However, the German and Gaulish (French) slaves among them refused to continue over the Alps. Instead of marching the rest of his army out of Italy to freedom, Spartacus responded by marching south again, with the intention of reaching the island of Sicily by ship from southern Italy.

The decision proved fatal. Spartacus agreed to a deal with a group of pirates, who said they would provide ships. However, they betrayed him, and no ships came. In 71 BCE Spartacus's forces were defeated by the army of Marcus Licinius Crassus. Under the orders of Crassus, every one of the six thousand survivors was crucified, as an example to other slaves of the consequences of rebellion. It is not known whether Spartacus was killed in the battle or was crucified.

Legacy

Soon after his death, Spartacus passed into legend—as a figure of fear for Romans and as a hero for the oppressed and the enslaved. His bravery, strength, and skill as a leader were enhanced by his reputation as a humane man who deplored the injustice of slavery and believed all men and women should be free.

SEE ALSO

Sports and Entertainment

Since long before the earliest written records, people have participated in a wide variety of sports and forms of entertainment. Many ancient peoples developed theatrical and musical entertainments. The earliest physical games and sporting contests seem to have arisen out of the need to improve prehistoric survival skills.

Running, jumping, and fighting were all essential skills during the early history of humanity, as people needed to hunt for food and flee from predators. Over thousands of years, these activities developed into some of the sports that are still watched and played.

Hunting and Fighting Sports

Some sports arose out of the need to practice and perfect hunting and fighting skills. For example, the need to fire bows and arrows or throw spears with accuracy and over great distances led to archery and javelin competitions.

From as early as 2500 BCE, people of the Indus valley civilization held regular sporting competitions involving weapons such as the *toran* (similar to the javelin) and the *chakra* (a form of discus).

Some sports were a test of bravery as much as athleticism. The Minoans, whose culture flourished from 2000 BCE, invented the sport of bull leaping, which involved the athlete—who could be either a man or a woman—clearing a bull that was rushing toward him or her by a combination of seizing its horns, flipping, and jumping. Spectacular and dangerous, it is considered a forerunner of bullfighting.

Weaponless Combat Sports

Many sporting contests developed out of one person's desire to test himself or herself against another person. Tests of strength and weaponless fights may have had a purpose other than entertainment or exercise in prehistoric times. In some cases such contests may have decided leadership of a tribe.

▲ *This Minoan ring, with a scene of bull leaping, dates from around 1500 BCE.*

Wrestling is believed to be one of the oldest of all recognizable sports. The ancient Sumerians wrestled for sport more than four thousand years ago. The oldest written record of a specific sports event was a wrestling contest between Egyptian and foreign soldiers, held in front of the pharaoh Ramses III in 1160 BCE.

Influenced by wrestling in both China and Korea, sumo wrestling developed in Japan between 300 and 200 BCE, while the ancient Egyptians and Mesopotamians boxed many centuries before it became an event in the ancient Greek Olympic games.

▶ *This marble sculpture shows the Greek hero Hercules wrestling with Achelous.*

Racing with Horses

The domestication of animals began in pre-historic times, as humans started to settle in one place and learned how to farm crops and rear animals for food and clothing. The taming and riding of horses is believed to have started in Arabia more than five thousand years ago. Racing horses or using them to pull chariots in races was a popular sport in many ancient civilizations.

Although chariot racing was a major feature of Roman games, chariots were raced many centuries earlier in Babylonia, Egypt, and ancient Greece. One of the most famous of all ancient charioteers was Cynisca. The daughter of the Spartan king Agesilaus II, she was the first woman known to have bred horses and, in 396 BCE, also the first to win at the ancient Olympics.

Roman Games

The first Roman games—involving a fight to the death between six slaves—were staged in 264 BCE by two men in honor of their dead father. The games grew so popular that giant amphitheaters, such as the Colosseum, were built to hold thousands of spectators.

What the spectators witnessed was a combination of processions; *venationes*, which were fights between men and wild animals (including elephants, lions, and other big cats); and brutal, bloody contests between gladiators.

Gladiators could be slaves, criminals, or freemen. Trained in gladiator schools, they fought with an array of different weapons, including nets, tridents (three-pronged spears), lances, swords, and shields. Most battles were to the death, although sometimes a defeated man's fate would be decided upon by the emperor or the crowd.

ANCIENT EGYPTIAN SPORTS

The sports most commonly depicted in Egyptian art are wrestling, boxing, stick fighting, archery, hunting, and chariot driving. To a lesser extent, Egyptians swam and played ball games.

Another extremely popular sport in ancient Egypt was a form of jousting on water. Rival groups of fishermen, propelling their rafts along with long poles, would find themselves competing for the same patch of water. Those on the bow of the boats would use their pole to push the other boats away or even to force fishermen on the other boats into the water. With several boats joining in at a time, this sport was boisterous, chaotic, and great fun, although tempers were easily inflamed and the fun could descend into plain fistfights.

Mayan Ball Courts

Few playing fields on which ancient sports were played have survived. Notable exceptions are the Mayan ball courts found in South and Central America. Surrounded by stone walls, the courts were often located near major religious temples. Experts believe that teams of Mayan males competed for a heavy ball, with the aim of passing the ball through a stone hoop to score or win the game outright. Behind the game lay much ritual and ceremony.

▲ *This scene from a tomb in Saqqara, Egypt, shows a mock fight between different crews on rafts made from papyrus reeds.*

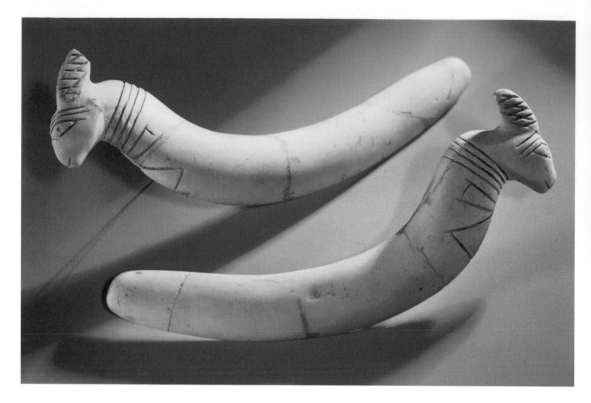

▶ *These Egyptian clappers, used as a percussion instrument, are made from hippopotamus ivory and date from between 3100 and 2700 BCE.*

It is thought that the Mayan ball game was linked to the return of spring. The ball may have represented the sun, the play from one side to another of the ball court representing sunrise and sunset. Scenes from Mayan artifacts appear to show losers being sacrificed as a gift to the gods.

Egyptian Musical Entertainment

Many ancient civilizations learned how to make music, particularly using the human voice and percussion instruments such as drums and cymbals.

Music was very important in ancient Egyptian society. Tomb and temple scenes show a variety of musical instruments, and many Egyptians were buried with instruments. Festivals were held in large settlements, and crowds of thousands would be entertained by large orchestras of musicians who played wind instruments such as flutes and pipes, stringed instruments such as lyres and harps, and percussion instruments, including drums and rattles. Another percussion instrument was a set of clappers made of bone, which were apparently used much as modern Spanish castanets are.

The musicians were often accompanied by male and female dancers, some of whom performed well-choreographed acrobatic moves.

MILO OF KROTON

One of the most famed athletes in the ancient world was the wrestler Milo of Kroton. Born in southern Italy, Milo won the boys' wrestling contest at the ancient Olympics in 540 BCE. He returned eight years later to win the first of five consecutive wrestling titles. According to legend, Milo would train and demonstrate his great strength and skill by standing on a greased disc of iron and challenging others to push him off.

SEE ALSO
• Colosseum • Egypt • Festivals • Games
• Music and Dance • Olympia

Glossary

amber A hard yellow resin used in jewelry and ornaments.

auxiliary An irregular soldier, one who fights only when called upon.

basilica A large oblong building with two rows of columns and an apse (a domed semicircular section).

bas-relief A type of sculpture in which the design projects slightly from a flat background.

broch A circular stone tower found in the coastal parts of northern and western Scotland and the nearby islands.

cairn A mound of stones created by human activity. Some are mounds made by farmers; others are mounds over graves or burial chambers.

chambered cairn A type of prehistoric tomb in which the burial chamber is covered by a mound, or cairn, of stones and soil.

Circus Maximus A U-shaped amphitheater in Rome where chariot races were held.

cupbearer A person who serves wine in a noble household.

edict An official command or announcement.

enlightenment Defined by Buddhists as a state of blissful peace involving freedom from ignorance and from attachment to worldly things.

galley A long, low-lying boat, propelled by oars or sails, used in ancient times, especially in the Mediterranean.

hemlock A poisonous plant; it was used as a method of capital punishment in ancient Athens.

hemp A plant whose coarse fibers can be used to make, cloth, rope, and a writing surface.

hull The framework of a ship.

joust A contest wherein two riders with lances try to unseat each other as they pass.

keel The V-shaped bottom of a ship.

legionary A Roman soldier who belonged to a force of around 5,500 men, called a legion; he served in the army for between twenty and twenty-five years.

menial Requiring little or no skill or thought; undignified.

metic A foreigner living and working in ancient Athens.

mildew A tiny fungus that forms a white coating on an object in damp conditions.

millet A fast-growing annual cereal plant grown for its seed and used for hay.

nomad Any one of a group of people that move from place to place seasonally in search of pasture for their herds or food and water.

oracle A shrine where ancient Greeks consulted a god for advice or a prophecy; also, the priestess through whom the god was thought to speak.

patrician A noble member of society.

persecution The practice of punishing people, often killing them, because of their race or religious or political beliefs.

reincarnation A central belief of Hinduism—that, after death, a person is born again into a new body.

sibyl In ancient times, a woman believed to foretell the future by becoming the mouthpiece of the god Apollo.

steppe A grassy treeless plain, particularly of the kind found in Russia.

stern The rear of a boat or ship.

stupa In Buddhism, a domed shrine.

suckle Feed young offspring with milk from udders or breasts.

toga A draped garment commonly worn by men in ancient Rome.

vassal A person, nation, or group that is dominated or occupied by another ruler or nation.

volume In mathematics, the amount of space filled by an object.

Index

Page numbers in **boldface type** refer to main articles.
Page numbers in *italic type* refer to illustrations.